RESEARCH PERSPECTIVES IN ACCOUNTING

RESEARCH PERSPECTIVES IN ACCOUNTING

Ahmed Riahi-Belkaoui

QUORUM BOOKS
Westport, Connecticut • London

Library of Congress Cataloging-in-Publication Data

Riahi-Belkaoui, Ahmed, 1943–
    Research perspectives in accounting / Ahmed Riahi-Belkaoui.
      p.   cm.
    Includes bibliographical references and index.
    ISBN 1–56720–100–8 (alk. paper)
     1. Accounting—Research—Methodology.   I. Title.
    HF5630.R53   1997
    657'.072—dc21   97–1697

British Library Cataloguing in Publication Data is available.

Library of Congress Catalog Card Number: 97–1697
ISBN: 1–56720–100–8

First published in 1997

Quorum Books, 88 Post Road West, Westport, CT 06881
An imprint of Greenwood Publishing Group, Inc.

Printed in the United States of America

The paper used in this book complies with the
Permanent Paper Standard issued by the National
Information Standards Organization (Z39.48–1984).

10 9 8 7 6 5 4 3 2

To Hedi and Janice

CONTENTS

Exhibits   ix

Preface   xi

1. Perspectives on Accounting Knowledge   1

2. Perspectives on Accounting Research   17

3. Perspectives on Accounting Paradigms   45

4. Perspectives on Standard Setting: The Essence of a Decision   69

5. Perspectives on Accounting Researchers and Methodologies   105

6. Perspectives on the Sociology of Academic Accountants   121

    Index   153

EXHIBITS

Exhibit 1.1:	World Hypotheses	2
Exhibit 1.2:	Reformulation of World Hypotheses	8
Exhibit 2.1:	Four Views for the Analysis of Social Theory	19
Exhibit 2.2:	Network of Basic Assumptions Characterizing the Subjective-Objective Debate Within Social Science	21
Exhibit 2.3:	Assumptions About Ontology and Human Nature	22
Exhibit 3.1:	Concepts of Equilibrium Periods in Six Theories	47
Exhibit 3.2:	Concepts of Deep Structure in Six Theories	48
Exhibit 4.1:	Summary of Model-Relevant Interpretations	96
Exhibit 5.1:	Kolb et al.'s Model of Human Learning	106
Exhibit 5.2:	The Relationships Between Epistemology, Methodology, Methods, and Knowledge	107
Exhibit 5.3:	Forms of Knowledge and the Learning Cycle	108
Exhibit 5.4:	Jungian's Typology of Researchers	109
Exhibit 5.5:	Alternative Modes of Inquiry	113
Exhibit 5.6:	Differences Between the Two Modes of Inquiry	114
Exhibit 6.1:	Expected Interrelations Among Value Dimensions: Second-Order Hypothesis	129
Exhibit 6.2:	Significant Factor Loadings	132
Exhibit 6.3:	Summary: Observed Versus Expected Factors	135
Exhibit 6.4:	Pure Accounting Theory (Factor 1)	136

Exhibit 6.5:   Scientific Method (Factor 2)   137

Exhibit 6.6:   Societal Role and Beliefs About People and Places (Factor 3)   138

Exhibit 6.7:   Self-Image (Factor 4)   139

Exhibit 6.8:   Professionalization (Factor 5)   140

Exhibit 6.9:   Worldviews (Factor 6)   141

Exhibit 6.10:   Value Freeness (Factor 7)   142

Exhibit 6.11:   Expected Versus Actual Relationships Among Factors   142

PREFACE

Accounting is a social science as evidenced by the quality and quantity of its research output and its researchers in the establishment of a political, social, and economic order. To reach this level of importance as a discipline, accounting had to diversify its approaches and output and to develop different perspectives or "visions" in the conduct and practice of research. These perspectives encompass accounting knowledge, accounting research, accounting paradigms, standard setting, accounting researchers and methodologies, and the sociology of academic accountants. It is the object of this book to explicate these different perspectives for a better understanding of the conduct, practice, and outcome of accounting research and knowledge.

The book will be of interest to practicing accountants, academics, businesspeople, students, legislators, social scientists, and others interested in better understanding of the conduct, practice, and outcomes of accounting research.

Many people have helped in the development of this book. I received considerable assistance from the University of Illinois at Chicago research assistants, especially Dimitra Alvertos and Hiral Patel. I also thank Eric Valentine and Katie Chase and the entire production team at Quorum Books for their continuous and intelligent support. Finally, to my entire family, thanks for making everything possible and enjoyable.

RESEARCH PERSPECTIVES IN ACCOUNTING

1
PERSPECTIVES ON ACCOUNTING KNOWLEDGE

Accounting research has taken various avenues leading to an array of innovative and diverse knowledge. The diversity of knowledge in accounting may appear to the novice as resisting synthesis. This chapter draws on Stephen Pepper's *World Hypotheses*[1] to provide four different approaches to obtaining and classifying formal knowledge in accounting: formism, mechanism, contextualism, and organicism. They are shown to be useful for a better understanding and appreciation of the ways of obtaining and interpreting accounting knowledge.

THE NATURE OF PEPPER'S FRAMEWORK

Formism relates to the realism of Plato, Aristotle, scholastics, neo-scholastics, neorealists, and Western realists. Mechanism relates to the naturalism or materialism of Democritus, Lucretius, Galileo, Descartes, Thomas Hobbes, John Locke, George Berkeley, David Hume, and Reichenbach. Contextualism relates to the pragmatism of Charles Pierce, William James, H.-L. Bergson, John Dewey, and George Mead. Finally organicism relates to the absolute or objective idealism of Friedrich Schelling, George Hegel, Thomas Green, Arthur Granville Bradley, Bernard Bosanquet and Josiah Royce.[2]

These sets of assumptions concerning the logical structure of the special world can be used to distinguish between the four world hypotheses, which are shown in Exhibit 1.1. A first dimension distinguishes between analytic theories and synthetic theories. A second dimension distinguishes

Exhibit 1.1
World Hypotheses

```
                            DISPERSE THEORIES


                                    |

                                    |

     CONTEXTUALISM                  |              FORMISM

(Root Metaphor: The Historic       |      (Root Metaphor:  Similarity)

  Event)                           |

                                   |

                                   |

                                   |


Synthetic ─────────────────────────┼───────────────────────────── Analytic

Theories                           |                              Theories

                                   |

                                   |

                                   |

                                   |

                                   |

     ORGANICISM                    |              MECHANISM

(Root Metaphor:  The Integrated    |      (Root Metaphor:  The Machine)

  Whole)                           |

                                   |

                                   |

                   Integrative Theories
```

between disperse theories and integrative theories. Basically analytic theories do not recognize and interpret synthesis, so that complexes or contexts are derivative, not an essential part of the organization. Synthetic theories are instead complexes or contexts so that analysis becomes derivative. Dispersive theories focus on interpretation of facts that are retrieved one by one from a universe of facts.

As stated by Pepper, "facts are taken one by one from whatever source they come and are interpreted as they come and so are left. The universe has for these theories the general effect of multitudes of facts rather loosely scattered about and not necessarily determining one another to any considerable degree.''[3] Dispersive theories are characterized by an inadequacy of precision while integrative theories are characterized by an inadequacy of scope. As a result of the use of these two dimensions, the four world hypothesis can be characterized as follows:

1. Formism includes analytic and dispersive theories.
2. Mechanism includes analytic and integrative theories.
3. Contextualism includes synthetic and dispersive theories.
4. Organicism includes synthetic and integrative theories.

Formism

As shown in Exhibit 1.1, formism includes both analytic and disperse theories. Its root metaphor is similarity. This assumes that formism focuses on phenomena—objects, events, processes—that are taken one by one from whatever source, and attempts to identify similarities or differences through a mere description and to accept the results of the description. The central activity is therefore description on the basis of similarities. There are three categories for the description on formism: (1) characters, (2) particulars, and (3) participation. If we state that "this is accounting," "this" is an uncharacterized particular; "accounting," the unparticularized character; and "is," the participation of one in the other to produce the object.[4]

Formism, or more precisely immanent formism, is therefore a particularization of a character or the characterization of a particular. The set of particulars or norms that participate in one or more characters is a class. For example, cash, accounts receivables, short-term inventories, and short-term investments that are liquid constitute the class of current assets. The classes can of course be classified in various ways. What appears in formism is that truth is the degree of similarity of a description to its object of reference. It is a truth theory based on correspondence. It does not include statements of empirical uniformities. As stated by Pepper:

From the point of view of a formist, statements of empirical uniformities are only half truths. Full truths are descriptions which accurately correspond with facts that have occurred or with laws that necessarily hold. Descriptions of empirical uniformities are simply rungs in the ladder from contingent fact to necessary law. They are signs of human ignorance. For if we knew the whole truth about them, we should know the law or the combinations of law which made their regularity necessary, or we should know that they were not necessary but were mere historical coincidences which have been mistakenly generalized and which cannot be relied upon for scientific predictions.[5]

Mechanism

As shown in Exhibit 1.1, mechanism includes both analytic and integrative theories. Its root metaphor is a machine. Like formism it is an analytic theory focusing on discrete elements rather than complexes or contexts. Unlike formism, however, it is integrative in the sense that the world is well-ordered and the "facts occur in a determinate order and where, if enough were known, they could be predicted, or at least described, as being necessarily as just what they are.[6] Six important points are made about mechanism:

1. Like a machine, the object of study is composed of parts having specified locations. As stated by Haridimos Tsoukas, "the object of study is regarded as ontologically given, fully describable, and algorithmically compressible. It is assumed to consist of discrete parts whose *locations* can be specified. In the case of a social object of study this means that its parts, as well as the relationships among them, can be represented in an abbreviated form."[7]

2. The parts can be expressed in quantitative form, which is different from the objects as viewed in their commonsense form. The quantitative measures are called primary qualities. Examples include size, shape motion, number, and so on.

3. A lawful relationship between the parts of the object of study is described by functional equations or statistical correlations.

4. In addition to the primary qualities, there are other characteristics that can be expressed quantitatively, although not directly relevant to the object of the study. *They are secondary qualities.*

5. The secondary qualities are also related by some principle to the object of the study.

6. The secondary qualities are also linked by stable relationships or secondary laws

These six features constitute the categories of mechanism as follows:

Primary Categories

1. Field of location
2. Primary qualities
3. Laws holding for configurations of primary qualities in the field (primary laws)

Secondary Categories

4. Secondary qualities
5. A principle for connecting the secondary qualities with the first three primary or effective categories
6. Laws, if any, for regularities among secondary qualities (secondary laws)[8]

Another good view of mechanism is provided by Jamshid Gharajedaghi and Russell Ackoff as follows:

Mechanistic models of the world conceptualize it as a machine that works with a regularity dictated by its internal structure and the causal laws of nature. The world, like a hermetically sealed clock, is taken to be made up of purposeless and passive parts that operate predictably. Any deviation from regularity is reacted to with changes that restore it; the system is believed to tend in the long run toward a static equilibrium.[9]

Its truth theory is based on causal adjustment, workability, and prediction: in effect, to find if the machine works.

Contextualism

As shown in Exhibit 1.1, contextualism includes both synthetic and disperse theories. Its root metaphor is the historical event. Like formism, contextualism is synthetic, in that it focuses on a pattern, a gestalt as the object of study rather than on disparate facts. Like formism, contextualism is dispersive in that the focus is on the interpretation of independent facts retrieved one by one from a universe of facts. These facts are characterized by continuously changing patterns, making *change* and *novelty* the ineradicable contextualistic categories. With the historical event as the root metaphor, every event is subject to change and novelty and is characterized at a given point in time by *quality* and *texture*, making them the basic categories of contextualism. Quality is characterized by the *spread* of an event, its *change* and its *degrees of fusion*. Texture is characterized by its *strands*, its *context*, and its *references*. Tsoukas offers the following explanation:

Quality is the intuited wholeness of an event: texture is the details and relations making up the quality. We understand events by grasping intuitively the whole pattern (a face, a mark, a song, a painting, etc.), and when we wonder why we are sure of our intuitions we start analyzing their texture.[10]

The truth theory of contextualism is operational in terms of qualitative confirmation and pragmatic working. Only verbs should be used in the language of contextualism: doing, enduring, enjoying, and so on. As stated by Roy Payne,

one of the major derivatives of such philosophical stance is that change is endemic. The context will change and thus knowledge will need to change also. Consequently the truth theory of contextualism is "qualitative confirmation" or verification, though such verification demands a thorough exploration of the context and texture of any event. Strictly speaking it is not the event but a hypothesis about the event that is verified, so hypotheses, not events, are regarded as being true or false.[11]

Later in another book, Pepper proposed selectivism as an expanded and radical revision of contextualism with a root metaphor of a goal-seeking or purposive act; and a theory of truth based on operational correspondence.[12]

Organicism

As shown in Exhibit 1.1, organicism includes both synthetic and integrative theories. Its root metaphor is the integrated whole. Like mechanism, it is integrated in the sense the world is composed of well-ordered and -integrated facts that can be described as well as predicted. Like contextualism, it is synthetic focusing in the gestalt as the object of study rather than disparate facts. Everything is considered to be coherent and well-integrated with seven features: (1) *fragments of experience* appearing with (2) *nexuses* or connections which spontaneously lead as a result of the aggravation of (3) *traditions*, gaps, opposition, or counteractions to resolution in (4) an *organic whole* (5) *implicit* in the fragments and (6) *transcending* the previous contradictions by means of a coherent totality, which (7) *economizes*, saves, and preserves all the original fragments of experience without any loss.[13]

Basically, organicism is concerned with the determination of an organic whole from connected and integrated fragments, in a kind of synthesis that recognizes the contradictions and integrates them in a more complete *holon*. The key is integration and comprehension culminating in a *telos*—that is, an ultimate, most inclusive structure.[14] The truth theory of organicism is coherence as based on determinateness and absoluteness. In other words, "organicism thus proposes the existence of degrees of truth dependent on the amount of facts known, and when all facts are known—as in principle they can be—then absolute truth has been obtained."[15]

Reformulation of World Hypotheses

Exhibit 1.2 shows a reformulation of the world hypotheses that can make their application to accounting research more salient and comprehensive. The exhibit still shows the two uses of synthetic to analytic theories and dispersive to integrative theories as well as the four hypotheses of formism, mechanism, contextualism, and organicism. In addition the exhibit has in each quadrant five different objects, events, processes, or phenomena.

In the formism quadrant the five objects are shown to be discrete objects of study and the researcher is only interested in identifying similarities and differences without an interest in the mechanism creating those similarities and differences. In the contextualism quadrant, the only difference with the situation in formism is that three facts are placed in one context and two are placed in another context. Each context now constitutes a pattern, a gestalt as the object of study rather than the disparate facts. Each context has quality and texture. In the mechanism quadrant, the only difference with formism is that the disparate facts can now be quantitatively described and related, allowing the study of linear relationships. In the organicism quadrant, the only difference from mechanism is that the quantitative relationships can be placed in a specific context to constitute an organic whole.

VISIONS IN ACCOUNTING KNOWLEDGE

Formism in Accounting

Those adopting formism in accounting are working for similarities and differences between different objects of study without any concern for potential relationships between them. It may be argued that all of the technical knowledge in accounting used in the teaching of accounting

Exhibit 1.2
Reformulation of World Hypotheses

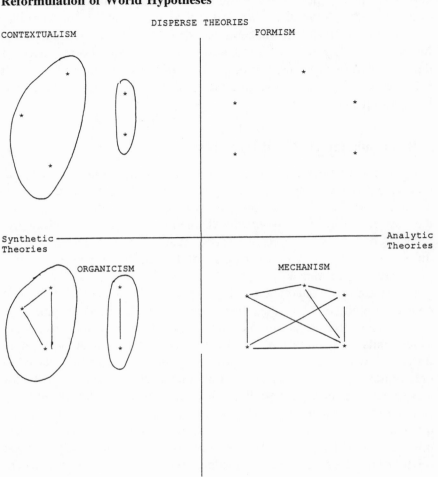

and included in standard textbooks is inescapably formistic to a great extent. The general rules, models, and algorithms used to explain accounting phenomena and to help in the conduct of accounting practice are discrete objects of study that can be compared in terms of the extent of similarities and differences between them. This aspect of the field of accounting is characterized by a relentless classification methodology.

Every aspect of accounting knowledge is subjected to typologies that are assumed to reflect the world as it is or as it should be. The inquiry of researchers in formism is focused on the taxonomic character of the object of study rather than the causes of similarities and differences. Formism fits well in accounting practice where categorization is tantamount to reaching solutions.[16] It is essential to the particularization of an accounting character or the characterization of an accounting character or the characterization of an accounting particular. It is a constant search for a "holy grail" of accounting, just as it is in such fields as zoology, botany, and chemistry.

Mechanism in Accounting

Those adopting mechanism in accounting not only are looking for similarities and differences between objects of study but also and mainly for quantitative relationships that allow both description and prediction. Mechanism in accounting is also the search of empirical regularities between different phenomena through various forms of statistical correlations. The objects of study are viewed as multidimensional as machines. We need to know the parts as well as the principles and relationships between the parts. This calls for operationalization of the discrete dimensions and description of the order that keeps them related.

Most of empirical research in accounting, or so-called mainstream research, is inescapably mechanistic to a great extent. Market research, behavioral research, positive accounting research, event prediction studies, and most correlation-based studies in mainstream accounting research reflect the analytical bent of mechanism by focusing on discrete phenomena, not complexes or contexts, and the integrative bent of mechanism by looking at the world as well-ordered with specific relationships that can be described and qualified. The result is lamentable because of (1) unsatisfactory level of correlation coefficients, (2) lack of control for alternative explanations, (3) unrepresentative samples, and (4) endless but "disguised" replications.

Similar remarks about mechanism have been made in organizational behavior,[17,18] and in industrial and organizational psychology.[19] But the real failure of mechanism results from the inordinately high amount of data required to guarantee the predictive power of a mechanistic type of knowledge, and the failure to transfer easily the knowledge to the actual world.[20]

All of this is contributing to friction among the establishments with the prospects of decreasing interdisciplinary relationships and a decline in the production of useful formal accounting knowledge. In the process

the scientific establishments in accounting may have created for themselves a self-made prison. And they would resist any appeal to escape
from their man-made trap because it runs counter to organized beliefs
and values. As Norbert Elias explains,

what is demanded of them is the re-framing of their problem and its solution in
terms which, in their eyes, have a lower cognitive status than their own. All
that, they may feel, is too high a price to pay for an escape from an intellectual
impasse so they prefer to stay in the homely trap of the insoluble problem and
to carry along from generation to generation the flag of a tradition which, though
it has little intrinsic cognitive value has, as one can well understand, a high
value for their representatives.[21]

The establishments rather control and engage in the production of their
brand of accounting formal knowledge. Their monopoly of that brand of
knowledge allows them to exclude others and/or to admit selectively only
those they can reproduce. In the process their brand of accounting knowledge suffers a professional deformation because it is merely used to
preserve their power and status, control entry into their field, and counteract other paradigms aiming for primacy in the field. The concerns of
these accounting academic elites are protection, discipline, and punish-
ment. To rely on Michel Foucault's terms,[22] the production of accounting
knowledge is never separate from the exercise of power. One result of
this situation is the constraining ideological influence on the production
of accounting knowledge. As expressed by C. E. Arrington and J. R.
Francis,

thus accounting research is less expansive and less intellectually rigorous than
it could be because of the disciplining forces of a hegemonic academic elite.
The theories proposed by this elite also reflect an extremely conservative political perspective on the role of accounting in producing the social order.[23]

Accounting knowledge is heading toward a crisis as a result of the
problems affecting its production by academic accountants and its use
by the accounting profession.

At the hands of academics the formal accounting knowledge is produced along
well-specified paradigms governed and controlled by well-established scientific
establishments. It is used, however, by the same academics as a tool to punish
and dominate, with scholarship losing ground to the need for power. In defend-
ing their particular paradigms and persisting in the defense of their restrictive

views, the same academics are at risk of creating self-made prisons that may hinder the production of quality accounting knowledge. At the same time in allying themselves with political power and policymaking they risk accelerating the deinstitutionalization and politicization of formal accounting knowledge. Caught in these scientific establishments and self-made prisons, accounting researchers may find themselves working on the same research path, contributing to a perpetual inquiry of the same issues without hope for closure.[24]

Contextualism in Accounting

Those adopting contextualism in accounting are focusing on the interpretation of independent facts drawn from a universe of facts under a specific context that would create a pattern or gestalt. The facts within each pattern are assumed to be subject to change and novelty. In addition they are distinguishable by their quality and texture. Because of the notion of change, the analysis under a specific context takes the ontological assumption that the social world or the accounting world is incessantly on the move. The fundamental difference between contextualism and formism in accounting is that the facts are now congregated into specific contexts. Therefore, it may be argued that the new accounting technical knowledge that is accumulated for specific contexts constitutes a good example of contextualism in accounting. Examples of the new contexts include (1) economic events, such as bankruptcy, takeovers, and bond ratings; (2) industry classification, and (3) temporal classification, such as before and after a major political, economic, or social event.

Every aspect of accounting knowledge can be classified under a grouping characterized by a specific context. One may consider the accounting techniques and the body of knowledge classified by industry. Their study is confined to a particular industry at a time. The reduction of the analysis from all the facts to a few facts pertinent to a particular context gives contextualism a more focused scope than formism. Case analyses and qualitative research in accounting and management studies with a focus on the creation of narratives and stories for the interpretation of unique episode are clear examples of contextualism.[25,26,27,28] In addition, most of the professional accounting literature written in lay language attempts to provide "how to" solutions in specific contexts to the general public and executives interested in using specific accounting problems in specific contexts. Contextualism appears to be more helpful to the practice of accounting than formism by working for a specific gestalt in accounting where it can pinpoint "what is useful" and "what is not useful," and can identify the working of specific organizational cultures in accounting.

Organicism in Accounting

Those adopting organicism in accounting are focusing on specific gestalts as objects of study that are composed of well-ordered and -integrated facts that can be described as well as predicted. Like mechanism in accounting, organicism seeks the determination of empirical regularities between different phenomena through various forms of statistical analysis. Unlike mechanism, the search for empirical regularities is reduced to specific contexts or gestalts. By doing so, organicism avoids most of the limitations of mechanism in accounting by integrating the research and findings around a specific context. For example, if the specific context is bankruptcy, mechanism will focus on generic models of bankruptcy while organicism will focus on specific models of bankruptcy in specific contexts such as a specific industry, a specific period of time, a specific country, and so on.

Organicism in accounting is viewed as an important factor of future accounting research. As stated by William Beaver,

a second factor is the emphasis on contextual rather than generic research. In part, it is implicit in the first factor where there is an emphasis on institutional richness which tends to lead to specific contexts. The value of generic studies is diminishing because prior research has reaped much of those gains and has already addressed the basic, first order questions—e.g., is there a statistical relation between returns and earnings changes? However, as the questions become more demanding or the effects are of a second order, there is an increased premium on increasing the power of the tests. This often dictates particular samples and specific reporting issues. In a related view, the contextual investigations will often require the collection of distinctive databases.[29]

Organicism in accounting will depend indeed on the availability of original databases that focus on specific contexts that will recognize the particularity of data and harmonize them in a more complete accounting *holon*, providing as a result more comprehensiveness and underlying structures.

CONCLUSION

The four world hypothesis of formism, mechanism, contextualism, and organicism are shown in this chapter to provide an ideal framework for an understanding of how accounting researchers obtain and classify accounting knowledge. The framework provides four visions of accounting knowledge, each resting on specific assumptions and understanding of accounting environments and research approaches.

NOTES

1. Stephen Pepper, *World Hypotheses: A Study in Evidence* (Berkeley: University of California Press, 1942).

2. Ibid., p. 141.

3. Ibid., pp. 142–43.

4. Ibid., p. 154.

5. Ibid., p. 183.

6. Ibid., p. 143.

7. Haridimos Tsoukas, "Refining Common Sense: Types of Knowledge in Management Studies," *Journal of Management Studies* (November 1994), p. 765.

8. Pepper, *World Hypotheses*, pp. 193–94.

9. Jamshid Gharajedaghi and Russell Ackoff, "Mechanisms, Organicisms and Social Systems," *Strategic Management Journal* 5 (1984), p. 290.

10. Tsoukas, "Refining Common Sense," p. 767.

11. Roy Payne, "The Nature of Knowledge and Organizational Psychology," in Nigel Nicholson and Toby D. Wall, eds., *The Theory and Practice of Organizational Psychology* (London: Academic Press, 1982), pp. 51–52.

12. S. C. Pepper, *Concept and Quality* (Chicago: Open Court, 1966).

13. Pepper, *World Hypotheses*, p. 769.

14. Tsoukas, "Refining Common Sense," p. 769.

15. Payne, "The Nature of Knowledge and Organizational Psychology," p. 52.

16. Ahmed Riahi-Belkaoui, *The Coming Crisis in Accounting* (Westport, CT: Greenwood Press, 1989).

17. R. Payne, "Truisms in Organizational Behaviour," *Interpersonal Development* 6 (1975/76), pp. 203–20.

18. L. Mohr, *Explaining Organizational Behavior* (San Francisco: Jossey-Bass, 1982).

19. J. Webster and W. Starbuck, "Theory Building in Industrial and Organizational Psychology," in C. Cooper and I. Robertson, eds., *International Review of Industrial and Organizational Psychology* (London: Wiley, 1988), pp. 93–138.

20. H. Tsoukas, "Introduction: From Social Engineering to Reflective Action in Organizational Behaviour," in H. Tsoukas, ed., *New Thinking in Organizational Behaviour* (Oxford: Butterworth/Heinemann, 1994), pp. 1–21.

21. Norbert Elias, "Scientific Establishments," in N. Elias and H. Martins, eds., *Scientific Establishments and Hierarchies* (Dordrecht, Holland: North-Holland, 1982), p. 31.

22. M. Foucault, *Power/Knowledge: Selected Interviews and Other Writings 1971–77*, ed. C. Gordon (New York: Random House, 1977).

23. C. E. Arrington and J. R. Francis, "Letting the Cat Out of the Bag: Deconstruction: Privilege and Accounting Research," *Accounting Organizations and Society* (January 1989), pp. 1–28.

24. Riahi-Belkaoui, *The Coming Crisis in Accounting*, p. 174.

25. M. K. Hunter, *Doctor's Stories* (Princeton, NJ: Princeton University Press, 1991).

26. K. Weick, "Organizational Cultures as a Source of High Reliability," *California Management Review* 26, (1987), pp. 112–27.

27. K. Weick and L. Browning, "Argument and Narration in Organizational Communication," *Journal of Management* 12 (1986), p. 62.

28. G. Morgan and L. Smircich, "The Case for Qualitative Research," *Academy of Management Review* 5 (1980), pp. 491–500.

29. William H. Beaver, "Directions in Accounting Research: Near and Far," *Accounting Horizons* (June 1996), p. 122.

SELECTED READINGS

Barrett, F. and S. Srivastava. (1991). "History as a Mode of Inquiry in Organizational Life: A Role for Human Cosmogony." *Human Relations* 44, pp. 231–54.

Burrell, G. and G. Morgan. (1979). *Sociological Paradigms and Organisational Analysis*. London: Heinemann.

Daft, R. and J. Wiginton. (1979). "Language and Organization." *Academy of Management Review* 4, pp. 179–91.

Evered, R. and M. R. Louis. (1981). "Alternative Perspectives in the Organizational Sciences: 'Inquiry from the Inside' and 'Inquiry from the outside.' " *Academy of Management Review* 6, pp. 385–95.

Foucault, M. (1971). "Orders of Discourse." *Social Science Information* 10, pp. 7–30.

Gersick, C. (1991). "Revolutionary Change Theories: A Multilevel Exploration of the Punctuated Equilibrium Paradigm." *Academy of Management Review* 16, pp. 10–36.

Macintyre, A. (1985). *After Virtue*, 2nd ed. London: Duckworth.

Miller, D. and P. Friesen. (1980). "Momentum and Revolution in Organizational Adaptation." *Academy of Management Journal* 23, pp. 591–614.

Mitroff, I. and R. Mason. (1982). "Business Policy and Metaphysics: Some Philosophical Considerations." *Academy of Management Review* 7, pp. 361–71.

Mohr, L. (1982). *Explaining Organizational Behavior*. San Francisco: Jossey-Bass.

Morgan, G. (1986). *Images of Organization*. London: Sage.

Morgan, G. (1980). "Paradigms, Metaphors and Puzzle-solving in Organization Theory." *Administrative Science Quarterly* 25, pp. 605–22.

Morgan, G. and L. Smircich. (1980). "The Case for Qualitative Research." *Academy of Management Review* 5, pp. 491–500.

Payne, R. (1982). "The Nature of Knowledge and Organizational Psychology." In Nigel Nicholson and Toby D. Wall, eds., *The Theory and Practice of Organizational Psychology*. London: Academic Press, pp. 37–67.

Payne, R. (1975/76). "Truisms in Organizational Behaviour." *Interpersonal Development* 6, pp. 203–20.

Pepper, S. (1942). *World Hypotheses: A Study in Evidence*. Berkeley: University of California Press.

Pettigrew, A. (1987). "Context and Action in the Transformation of the Firm." *Journal of Management Studies* 24, pp. 650–70.

Pettigrew, A. (1990). "Longitudinal Field Research on Change: Theory and Practice." *Organization Science* 1, pp. 267–92.

Rorty, R. (1991). *Objectivism, Relativism, and Truth*. Cambridge: Cambridge University Press.

Tsoukas, H. (1993a). "Analogical Reasoning and Knowledge Generation in Organization Theory." *Organization Studies* 14, pp. 323–46.

Tsoukas, H. (1993b). "Beyond Social Engineering and Contextualism: The Narrative Structure of Organisational Knowledge." Warwick Business School Research Paper No. 69. Warwick University.

Tsoukas, H. (1994). "Introduction: From Social Engineering to Reflective Action in Organizational Behaviour." In H. Tsoukas ed., *New Thinking in Organizational Behaviour*. Oxford: Butterworth/Heinemann, 1–21.

Tsoukas, H. (1991). "The Missing Link: A Transformational View of Metaphors in Organizational Science." *Academy of Management Review* 16, pp. 566–85.

Tsoukas, H. (1992). "The Relativity of Organizing: Its Knowledge Presuppositions and Its Pedagogical Implications for Comparative Management." *Journal of Management Education* 16, Special Issue, pp. S147–S162.

Weick, K. (1987). "Organizational Cultures as a Source of High Reliability." *California Management Review* 26, pp. 112–27.

Weick, K. and L. Browning. (1986). "Argument and Narration in Organizational Communication." *Journal of Management* 12, pp. 243–59.

Whitley, R. (1984a). "The Fragmented State of Management Studies: Reasons and Consequences." *Journal of Management Studies* 21, pp. 331–48.

Whitley, R. (1984b). "The Status of Management Research as a Practically-Oriented Social Science." *Journal of Management Studies* 21, pp. 369–90.

2
PERSPECTIVES ON
ACCOUNTING RESEARCH

Accounting research is elective and diverse. To the novice it may appear that accounting researchers are muddling through in their search of topics, methodology, and type of discourse. The realty is much different. Like every other social science, accounting conducts its research based upon assumptions about the nature of social science and the nature of society. An approach that has been applied by Gibson Burrell and Gareth Morgan to organizational analysis can be used to differentiate between four visions of research in accounting—the functionalist view, the interpretive view, the radical humanist view, and the radical structuralist view.[1] In this chapter they are explicated and applied to accounting research.

BURRELL AND MORGAN'S FRAMEWORK

The Nature of Social Science

Four assumptions about the nature of social science are examined as they relate to ontology, epistemology, human nature, and methodology. These assumptions also can be thought of in terms of the subjective-objective dimension.

First, the ontological assumption, concerning the very essence of the accounting phenomenon, involves nominalism-realism differences. The debate is whether the social world external to the individual cognition is a compound of pure names, concepts, and labels that give a structure to reality as in normalism, or whether it is a compound of real, factual, and tangible structures as in realism.

Second, the epistemological debate, concerning the grounds of knowledge and the nature of knowledge, involves the antipositivism-positivism debate. This debate focuses on the utility of a search for laws or underlying regularities in the field of social affairs. Positivism supports the utility. Antipositivism refutes it and argues for individual participation as a condition of understanding the social world.

Third, the human-nature debate, concerning the relationship between human beings and their environment, involves the voluntarism-determinism debate. This debate focuses on whether humans and their activities are determined by the situation or environment as in determinism, or are the result of their free will as in voluntarism.

Fourth, the methodology debate, concerning the methods used to investigate and learn about the social world, involves the ideographic-nomothetic debate. This debate focuses on whether the methodology involves the analysis of the subjective accounts obtained by participating or getting inside the situation as in the ideographic method, or whether it involves a rigorous and scientific testing of hypotheses as in the nomothetic method.

The Nature of Society

One assumption about the nature of society is made—namely, the order-conflict debate or, more precisely, the regulation-radical change debate. The *sociology of regulation* attempts to explain society by focusing on its unity and cohesiveness and the need for regulation. The *sociology of radical change*, in contrast, seeks to explain society by focusing on radical change, deep-seated structural conflict, modes of domination, and the structural contradictions of modern society. As highlighted by Burrell and Morgan, the sociology of regulation is concerned with status quo, social order, consensus, social integration and cohesion, solidarity, need satisfaction, and actuality, whereas the sociology of radical change is concerned with radical change, structural conflict, models of domination, contradiction, emancipation, deprivation, and potentiality.[2]

The Framework for Analysis of Research

As described earlier, any social science discipline, including accounting, can be analyzed along metatheoretical assumptions about the nature

Exhibit 2.1
Four Views for the Analysis of Social Theory

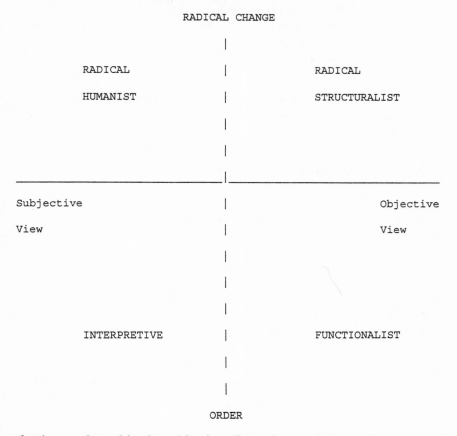

```
                        RADICAL CHANGE

                             |

        RADICAL              |              RADICAL

        HUMANIST             |              STRUCTURALIST

                             |

                             |

    _____|_____


   Subjective                |                         Objective

   View                      |                         View

                             |

                             |

                             |

        INTERPRETIVE         |              FUNCTIONALIST

                             |

                             |

                           ORDER
```

of science, the subjective-objective dimension, and about the nature of
society, the dimension of regulation-radical change. Using these two dimensions, Burrell and Morgan were able to develop a coherent scheme
for the analysis of social theory in general and organizational analysis
in particular.[3] The scheme consists of four distinct paradigms labeled as
(1) the radical humanist, characterized by the radical change and subjective dimensions; (2) the radical structuralist, characterized by the radical
change and objective dimensions; (3) the interpretive, characterized by
the subjective and regulation dimensions; and (4) the functionalist, characterized by the objective and regulation dimensions. The framework is
illustrated in Exhibit 2.1. It constitutes four views of reality to be used
in analyzing a wide range of social theories including accounting. As
Burrell and Morgan stated,

given the cross linkages between rival intellectual traditions, it becomes clear to us that our two sets of assumptions could be counter-posed to produce an analytical scheme for studying social theories in general. . . . we found that we possessed an extremely powerful tool for negotiating our way through different subject areas, and one which made sense of a great deal of the confusion which characterizes much contemporary debate within the social sciences.[4]

For example, the framework was used by Morgan to examine how organizational theory is influenced by its own assumptions through references to paradigms, metaphors, and puzzle-solving behavior. The assumptions, paradigms, metaphors, and related schools of organizational analysis are shown in Exhibits 2.2 and 2.3.

THE FRAMEWORK APPLIED IN THE SOCIAL SCIENCES

The Functionalist View in the Social Sciences

As defined earlier, the functionalist paradigm derives from the two perspectives of the sociology of regulation and objectivism. Functionalists are interested in explaining the social order from a realist, positivist, determinist, and nomothetic standpoint. They assume that social systems have a concrete, objective existence aimed at fostering purposeful behavior and an orderly, patterned social order. The general scope of the functionalist paradigm

seeks to provide . . . rational explanations of social affairs. It is . . . highly pragmatic in orientation, . . . It is often problem-oriented in approach, . . . It is usually firmly committed to a philosophy of social engineering as a basis of social change and emphasizes the importance of understanding order, equilibrium and stability in society. . . . It is concerned with the effective ''regulation'' and control of social affairs.[5]

The functionalist paradigm derives from the natural sciences from which it borrows models and methods. It traces its origins and intellectual tradition to Auguste Comte (1798–1857) and his emphasis on the positive model of the natural sciences, Herbert Spencer (1820–1903) and his study of sociology as the study of evolution in its most complex form and his impact on structural functionalism, Emile Durkheim (1858–1917)

Exhibit 2.2
Network of Basic Assumptions Characterizing the Subjective-Objective Debate Within Social Science

	Subjectivist Approaches to Social Science					Objectivist Approaches to Social Science
Core Ontological Assumptions	reality as a projection of human imagination	reality as a social construction	reality as a realm of symbolic discourse	reality as a contextual field of information	reality as a concrete process	reality as a concrete structure
Assumptions About Human Nature	man as pure spirit, consciousness, being	man as a social constructor, the symbol creator	man as an actor, the symbol user	man as an information processor	man as an adaptor	man as a responder
Basic Epistemological Stance	to obtain phenomenological insight, revelation	to understand how social reality is created	to understand patterns of symbolic discourse	to map contexts	to study systems, process, change	to construct a positivist science
Some Favored Metaphors	transcendental	language game, accomplishment, text	theater, culture	cybernetic	organism	machine
Research Methods	exploration of pure subjectivity	hemeneutics	symbolic analysis	contextual analysis of Gestalten	historical analysis	lab experiemnts, surveys

Source: Gareth Morgan and Linda Smircich, "The Case for Qualitative Research," *Academy of Management Review* 5, no. 4 (1980). p. 492. Reprinted with permission.

Exhibit 2.3
Assumptions About Ontology and Human Nature

	Reality as a Projection of Human Imagination	Reality as a Social Construction	Reality as Symbolic Discourse
CORE ONTOLO-GICAL ASSUMP-TIONS	The social world and what passes as "reality" is a projection of individual consciousness, it is an act of creative imagination and of dubious intersubjective status. This extreme position, commonly known as solipsism, asserts that there may be nothing outside oneself: one's mind is one's world. Certain transcendental approaches to phenomenology assert a reality in consciousness, the manifestation of a phenomenal world, but not necessarily accessible to understanding in the course of everyday affairs. Reality in this sense is masked by those human processes which judge and interpret the phenomenon in consciousness prior to a full understanding of the structure of meaning it expresses. Thus the nature of the phenomenal world may be accessible to the human being only through consciously phenomenological modes of insight.	The social world is a continuous process, created afresh in each encounter of everyday life as individuals impose themselves on their world to establish a realm of meaningful definition. They do so through the medium of language, labels, actions, and routines, which constitute symbolic modes of being in the world. Social reality is embedded in the nature and use of these modes of symbolic action. The realm of social affairs thus has no concrete status of any kind; it is a symbolic construction. Symbolic modes of being in the world, such as through the use of language, may result in the development of shared, but multiple realities, the status of which is fleeting, confined only to those moments in which they are actively constructed and sustained.	The social world is a pattern of symbolic relationships and meanings sustained through a process of human action and interaction. Although certain degree of continuity is preserved through the operation of rule-like activities that define a particular social milieu, the pattern is always open to reaffirmation or change through the interpretations and actions of individual members. The fundamental character of the social world is embedded in the network of subjective meanings that sustain the rule-like actions that lend it enduring form. Reality rests not in the rule or in rule-following, but in the system of meaningful action that renders itself to an external observer as rule-like.
ASSUMP-TIONS ABOUT HUMAN NATURE	Humans as Transcendental Beings Humans are viewed as intentional beings, directing their psychic energy and experience in ways that constitute the world in a meaningful, intentional form. There are realms of being, and realms of reality, constituted through different kinds of founding acts, stemming from a form of transcendental consciousness. Human beings shaped the world within the realm of their own immediate experience.	Humans Create Their Realities Human beings create their realities in the most fundamental ways, in an attempt to make their world intelligible to themselves and to others. They are not simply actors interpreting their situations in meaningful ways, for there are no situations other than those which individuals bring into being through their own creative activity. Individuals may work together to create a shared reality, but that reality is still a subjective construction capable of disappearing the moment its members cease to sustain it as such. Reality appears as real to individuals because of human acts of conscious or unwitting collusion.	Humans as Social Actors Human beings are social actors interpreting their milieu and orienting their actions in ways that are meaningful to them. In this process they utilize language, labels, routines for impression management, and other modes of culturally specific action. In so doing they contribute to the enactment of reality, human beings live in a world of symbolic significance, interpreting and enacting a meaningful relationship with that world. Humans are actors with the capacity to interpret, modify, and sometimes create the scripts that they play upon life's stage.
SOME EXAMPLES OF RESEARCH	Phenomenology	Ethnomethodology	Social Action Theory

22

Exhibit 2.3 (Continued)

Reality as a Contextual Field of Information	Reality as a Concrete Process	Reality as a Concrete Structure
The social world is a field of ever-changing form and activity based on the transmission of information. The form of activity that prevails at any one given time reflects a pattern of "difference" sustained by a particular kind of information exchange. Some forms of activity are more stable than others, reflecting an evolved pattern of learning based on principles of negative feedback. The nature of relationships within the field is probabilistic; a change in the appropriate pattern and balance within any sphere will reverberate throughout the whole, initiating patterns of adjustment and readjustment capable of changing the whole in fundamental ways. Relationships are relative rather than fixed and real.	The social world is an evolving process, concrete in nature, but ever-changing in detailed form. Everything interacts with everything else and it is extremely difficult to find determinate causal relationships between constituent processes. At best, the world expresses itself in terms of general and contingent relationships between its more stable and clear-cut elements. The situation is fluid and creates opportunities for those with appropriate ability to mold and exploit relationships in accordance with their interests. The world is in part what one makes of it: a struggle between various influences, each attempting to move toward achievement of desired ends.	The social world is a hard, concerete, real thing "out there," which affects everyone in one way or another. It can be thought of as a structure composed of a network of determinate relationships between constituent parts. Reality is to be found in the concrete behavior and relationships between these parts. It is an objective phenomenon that lends itself to accurate observation and measurement. Any aspect of the world that does not manifest itself in some form of observable activity or behavior must be regarded as being of questionable status. Reality by definition is what which is external and real. The social world is as concrete and real as the natural world.

Human as Information Processors	Humans as Adaptive Agents	Humans as Responding Machinisms
Human beings are engaged in a continual process of interaction and exchange with their context--receiving, interpreting, and acting on the information received, and in so doing creating a new pattern of information that effects changes in the field as a whole. Relationships between individual and context are constantly modified as a result of this exchange; the individual is but an element of a changing whole. The crucial relationship between individual and context is reflected in the pattern of learning and mutual adjustment that has evolved. Where this is well developed, the field of relationships is harmonious; where adjustment is low, the field is unstable and subject to unpredictable and discontinuous patterns of change.	Human beings exist in an interactive relationship with their world. They influence and are influenced by their context or environment. The process of exchange that operates here is essentially a competitive one, the individual seeking to interpret and exploit the environment to satisfy important needs, and hence survive. Relationships between individuals and environment express a pattern of activity necessary for survival and well-being of the individual.	Human beings are a product of the external forces in the environment to which they are exposed. Stimuli in their environment condition them to behave and respond to events in predictable and determinate ways. A network of causal relationships links all important aspects of behavior to context. Though human perception may influence this process to some degree, people always respond to situations in a lawful (i.e., rule-governed) manner.

Cybernetics	Open Systems Theory	Behaviorism Social Learning Theory

Source: Gareth Morgan and Linda Smircich, "The Case for Qualitative Research," *Academy of Management Review* 5, no. 4 (1980), pp. 494–95. Reprinted with permission.

23

and his notion of the objective reality of social facts, and Vilfredo Pareto (1848–1923) and his equilibrium model of society, to name only a few.

Within the functionalist paradigm in sociology, four theories or thoughts emerge: (1) social-system theory, (2) interactionism and social-action theory, (3) integrative theory, and (4) objectivism. They are defined as follows:

Social-system theory emerged as the pure picture of positivism arguing for the adoption of mechanical and biological systems for the study of sociology. It includes two schools of thought: structural functionalism and systems theory.

Structural functionalism, as exemplified in the works of social anthropologists Bronislaw Malinowski (1884–1942) and Alfred Radcliffe-Brown (1881–1955), focuses on establishing the functions that various elements of society perform, with the main argument that the ongoing life of a society may be perceived in terms of the functioning of its structure. As exemplified in the works of Talcott Parsons (1902–1979) and his analysis of the social system, it focuses on the "functional prerequisites" or "functional imperatives," the functions that may be achieved in order for a society to exist, and the adaptation, goal attainment, integration, and latency or pattern maintenance (AGIL scheme). It identifies the students or elements of social systems that serve given imperatives.

Systems theory is about the organization of complex elements standing in interactions. It consists of a selection of particular types of analogy to represent the system and a systems analysis. The analogy is either to mechanical, organism, or morphogenic models that are characteristic of the functionalist notions of order and stability. The systems analysis is aimed at revealing the principles of organization of the system.

The system approach is evident in the works of Ludwig von Bertalanffy ("General Systems Theory," 1956), Talcott Parsons (*The Social System*, 1951), G. C. Homans (*The Human Group*, 1950), Daniel Katz and Robert L. Kahn (*The Social Psychology of Organizations*, 1966), David Easton (*The Political System*, 1953), and Walter Buckley (*Sociology and Modern Systems Theory*, 1967).

Interactionism and social-action theory contain characteristics shared by both idealism and positivism. *Interactionism*, as exemplified in the works of Georg Simmel (1858–1918) and George Herbert Mead (1863–1931), focuses on an analysis of human association and interaction. Basically, the scope of social affairs is a process best characterized by social interaction. Its dominant form—*symbolic interactionism*—focuses on the interpretation of the meanings of actions or remarks and definition of the proper actions. People interpret other people's acts and convey to them how they should act. Symbolic interactionism is not, however, a coherent school of thought, since it may be differentiated into behavioral interactionism and phenomenological interactionism. The first assumes a view of a person living in a realist world of symbolic and physical objects that he or she responds to and tries to influence. The second assumes a view of a person constructing his or her environment on the basis of the person's ongoing activities.

Social-action theory, as exemplified in the works of Max Weber (1864–1920), focuses on "meaningful social action" as the ultimate object matter of sociology. Weber proposed a typology of rational, e-valuative, affectional, and traditional types of action for social analysis. Recurring actions may be used to discern the patterns of social relations or social structure.

Integrative theory is a term used to characterize the middle ground within the functionalist paradigm and includes four variations: P. M. Blau's exchange and power model as a source of integration, the Mertonian theory of the functions performed by elements of social and cultural structure, positive conflict functionalism, and the importance of information transmission in the morphogenic systems theory.[6]

Objectivism is characterized by a heavy commitment to the models and methods used in the natural sciences. It includes behaviorism and abstracted empiricism. *Behaviorism*, as reflected in the work of B. F. Skinner, focuses on an analysis of stimulus and response to develop causal theories of behavior. *Abstracted empiricism* is exemplified by the works of researchers who have allowed methodologies derived from the natural sciences to dominate their work.

The Interpretive View in the Social Sciences

As defined earlier, the interpretive paradigm derives from the two perspectives of the sociology of regulation and subjectivism. Interpretivists are interested in explaining the social order from a nominalist, antipositivist, voluntarist, and ideographic standpoint. They seek to understand the subjective experience of individuals. The general scope of the interpretive paradigm has been stated as follows:

It sees the social world as an emergent social process which is created by the individuals concerned. Social reality, . . . is regarded as being little more than a network of assumptions and intersubjectively shared meanings. The ontological status of the social world is viewed as extremely questionable and problematic. . . . Everyday life is accorded the status of a miraculous achievement. Interpretive philosophers and sociologists seek to understand the very basis and source of social reality.[7]

The interpretive view derives from the German idealist tradition of social thought as laid down by Immanuel Kant and as revived by Wilhelm Dilthey, Max Weber, Edmund Husserl, and Alfred Schutz. The concern shifted from the natural sciences with their emphasis on the investigation of the external process in a material world to the cultural sciences with their emphasis on the investigation of the internal process of human minds. The notion of *verstehen* (understanding) was used as the method to study the world of human affairs by reliving or reenacting the experience of others. It traces its organic and intellectual traditions to Dilthey (1833–1911) for its application to hermeneutics, to Husserl (1859–1938) for its application to phenomenology, and to Weber for its application to "interpretive sociology."

Within the interpretive paradigm in sociology, four theories or thoughts emerge: hermeneutics, solipsism, phenomenology, and phenomenological society, which are defined as follows:

Hermeneutics is concerned with a study of the objectifications of the human mind, like institutions, works of art, literature, languages, and religion, using the method of *verstehen*. It was characterized by Dilthey as follows:

Re-creating and re-living what is alien and past shows clearly how understanding rests on special, personal inspiration. But, as this is a significant and permanent condition of historical science, personal inspiration becomes a technique which develops with the development of historical consciousness. It is dependent on permanently fixed expressions being available so that understanding can always return to them. The methodical understanding of permanently fixed expressions we call exegesis. As the life of the mind only finds its complete, exhaustive and, therefore, objectively comprehensible expression in language, exegesis culminates in the interpretation of the written records of human existence. This method is the basis of philology. The science of this method is hermeneutics.[8]

H. G. Gadamer took the hermeneutic tradition one more step by focusing on language as an expression of the human mode.[9]

Solipsism, as exemplified in the works of the Irish cleric Bishop George Berkeley (1685–1753), takes the extreme subjective position by denying that the world has any distinct independent reality. It creates a situation of complete relativism and skepticism and therefore fails to make any important contribution to the social sciences.

Phenomenology can be divided into transcendental phenomenology and existential phenomenology. *Transcendental phenomenology*, as exemplified in the works of Edmund Husserl, focuses on the primacy of consciousness and subjective meaning in the interpretation of social action. To do this, the research must perform *epoche*—that is, to see if the substance of one's life world can be suspended. Only then can the fundamental and abstract properties of consciousness be exposed and understood, and then with the understanding of these properties real insight in the nature of reality would be possible. As P. A. Thevanaz put it,

Phenomenology is never an investigation of external or internal facts. On the contrary, it silences experience provisionally, leaves the question of objective reality or of real content aside in order to turn its attention solely and simply on the *reality in consciousness*, on the objects insofar as they are intended by and in consciousness, in short of what Husserl calls ideal essences. By this we must not understand mere subjective representations (which would leave us on the plane of psychology) nor ideal *realities* (which would "reify" or hypostasise unduly the data of consciousness and would put us on the level of metaphysics), but precisely the "phenomena." . . . The phenomena here is that which manifests itself immediately in consciousness; it is grasped in an invitation that precedes any reflection or any judgment. It has only to be allowed to show itself, to manifest itself; the *phenomenon* is that which gives itself (*Selbstgebring*). The phenomenological method then, faced with the objects and the contents of knowledge, consists in neglecting what alone counts for philosophers and scientists, namely their value, their reality or unreality. It consists in describing them such as they give themselves, as pure and simple intentions (*visles*) of consciousness, as meanings, to render them visible and manifest as such. In this *Wesenschar*, the essence (*Wesen*) is neither ideal *reality* nor psychological reality, but ideal intention (*visce*), intentional object of consciousness, imminent to consciousness.[10]

Existential phenomenology, as exemplified in the work of Alfred Schutz (1899–1959), departed from Husserl's strategy of holding the individual in radical abstraction and of searching for "pure mind" or the abstract laws of consciousness and adopted Weber's strategy of sympathetic introspection (*Verstehen*) into people's consciousness. This allowed phenomenology to move from philosophy to sociology to develop a "phenomenology of the social world" and to study empirically the creation and maintenance of intersubjectivity—that is, a common subjective world among pluralities of interacting individuals.

Phenomenological sociology can be divided into ethnomethodology and phenomenological symbolic interactionism. *Ethnomethodology* focuses on people's efforts to create a common sense of social reality. It attempts to discover and describe the set of rules and guidelines that people use to initiate behavior, respond to behavior, and modify behavior in social settings. It provides information about a society's unwritten rules for social behavior, and no behavior is too small for its scrutiny. To do these things it treats every happening as a topic of empirical study by focusing on "indexicality" and "reflexivity." Much human interaction is reflexive in that it has meaning in a particular context:

Everyday activities are seen as being ordered and rationally explicable within the context in which they occur. . . . The social situation is viewed as a process of accountable action which is sustained by the efforts of the participants. . . . [11]

Phenomenological symbolic interactionism was examined earlier when symbolic interactionism was distinguished in terms of behavioral and phenomenological.

The Radical Humanist View in the Social Sciences

The radical humanist view derives from the two perspectives of radical change and subjectivism. The radical humanist focuses on the notion that the individual creates the world in which he or she lives and tries to change it to escape alienation or false consciousness. This person views the social world from a nominalist, antipositivist, voluntarist, and ideographic perspective and places emphasis on radical change, modes of domination, emancipation, deprivation, and potentiality. The general scope of the radical humanist view

is underwritten by a common concern for the freedom of human spirit. . . . There tends to be a concern with . . . the pathology of consciousness, by which men . . . see themselves as trapped within a mode of social organization which they both create and sustain in their everyday lives. Radical humanists are concerned with understanding [how] this occurs, . . . to [set] human consciousness or spirit free and thus facilitat[e] the growth and development of human potentialities.[12]

The radical humanist view derives largely from Hegelianism and Hegel's view of individual consciousness as a focal point for the understanding of the nature of the social world and the dialectical relationship between consciousness and the external world. It influenced the young Karl Marx (1818–1883) in starting the foundation for the development of a radical humanism in the objective idealist world.

Within the radical humanist paradigms in sociology, four schools of thought emerge: (1) solipsism, (2) French existentialism, (3) critical theory, and (4) anarchistic individualism.

Solipsism, as discussed earlier in the interpretive paradigm, is an extreme approach.

French existentialism is best exemplified by the works of Jean-Paul Sartre (*Being and Nothingness*, 1966; *Existentialism and Humanism*, 1948; *Critique of Dialectical Reason*, 1976). Existentialism is the conviction that "existence comes before essence," which makes the individual rather than the essence of the real world the most important concern. Of importance are Sartre's three concepts of "models of being"; "being-in-itself" (*en-soi*), which reflects the external reality; "being-for-self" (*pour-soi*), which reflects consciousness and the intersubjectivity of humans; and finally, "being-for-others." The separation or gap between the first two modes of being is called "nothingness," which allows people to think of any nonobjects. The conception of "nothingness" endows the person with freedom. The reduction of "nothingness" by outside or self-imposed constraints leads to a situation of "bad faith" similar to Marx's concept of alienation.

Critical theory, as based on the work of the young Marx and as represented by the Frankfurt School of social theory, represents in fact three discrete schools of thought: Lukacsian sociology, Gramsci's sociology, and the Frankfurt School.

Lukacsian sociology, as based on the works of Georg Lukacs (1855–1974), seeks to provide a critical theory as an alternative to orthodox Marxism. The proletariat and its class consciousness became central to the overthrow of capitalist society. Men are seen as separate from the objectified things they create. This separation, or reification, is a form of alienation to be overcome by the proletariat.

Gramsci's sociology, as based on the works of Antonio Gramsci (1891–1937), seeks to develop a "philosophy of praxis" as a political methodology for the working class and as a total worldview, oriented to action and radical change.

The Frankfurt School is a generic title for the works of members like

Marx Horkheimer, Theodor Adorno, Walter Benjamin, Erich Fromm, Leo Lowenthal, Herbert Marcuse, and Jurgen Habermas. They have subjected most aspects of capitalist society to close intellectual scrutiny from a radical humanist perspective, including positivist science, modes of rationality, technology, the legal system, the family unit, patterns of bureaucracy, language, art, music, literature, the authoritarian personality, and psychoanalysis. For example, critical theory has been applied to organization science as an attempt to reject any science that reduces philosophical critique to some normative methodology. Here is a definition of critical theory as applied to organizational science:

Critical theory claims to be an empirical and practical philosophy which incorporates epistemological concerns such as the relationship between method and theory and the social consequences of theory validated through particular modes of research into methodology. As such, it requires two forms of analysis: a) a taxonomic analysis of the ontological, epistemological, and methodological concerns underlying organization science; and b) a critique (based on this analysis) of the dynamic interplay between organizational research, theory and practice.[13]

Anarchistic individualism advocates total individual freedom unhampered by any form of external or internal regulation. Like solipsism, it is an extreme view of the paradigm.

The Radical Structuralist View in the Social Sciences

As defined earlier, the radical structuralist paradigm derives from the two perspectives of the sociology of radical change and objectivism. Radical structuralists are interested in challenging the social order from a realist, positivist, deterministic, and nomothetic standpoint. They are committed to radical change, emancipation, and potentiality with an analysis emphasizing structural conflict, modes of domination, contradiction, and deprivation. The general scope of the radical structuralist paradigm has been stated as follows:

The paradigm reflects a sociology of radical change in which the idyllic vision of non-violent revolution through consciousness, such as that envisaged by many radical humanists, is left far behind. From the standpoint of radical structuralism, change in society almost inevitably involves a transformation of structures which, even given favorable circumstances, do not fall or change of their own accord. Structures are seen as being changed, first and foremost, through economic or political crises, which generate conflicts of such intensity that the *status quo* is necessarily disrupted or torn apart and replaced by radically different social forms.[14]

The radical structuralist paradigm derives from the work of Karl Marx and a materialistic view of nature and the social world. Marx distinguished between the economic base of society, or substructure, and the noneconomic base, or superstructure, and the contradictions between and within them. These contradictions become central to the explanation of changes in forms of society arising from continuous crises. Subsequent development to Marx's rule included (1) Friedrich Engels' interpretation of Marx and the birth of a "scientific socialism" in the Russian world, known as Marxism and consisting of a total science of man's political, economic, and social life; (2) V. I. Lenin and his followers' work standing between the critical theory of radical humanism and the tradition of orthodox Russian Marxism; and (3) Weber's work, or "radical Weberianism," with his analysis of bureaucracy, authority, and power as instruments of social domination best expressed as the "iron cage of bureaucracy."

Within the radical structuralist view in sociology, three theories or thoughts emerge: Russian social theory, contemporary Mediterranean Marxism, and conflict theory. *Russian social theory* covers N. I. Bukharin's Orthodox Marxism, or historical materialism, and P. A. Kropotkin's anarchistic communism. *Contemporary Mediterranean Marxism* covers Althusserian sociology from the works of Louis Althusser and Lucio Colletti's sociology. *Conflict theory* derives from the radical Weberianism and Weber's focus on a dominating role of bureaucracy, Ralf Dahrendorf's theory of society classes and class conflict, and John Rex's conflict theory.

THE FRAMEWORK APPLIED TO ACCOUNTING RESEARCH AND THEORY

Accounting theories and research have been based predominantly on the functionalist view, although modest attempts have been made to move to the interpretive, radical humanist, and radical structuralist paradigms.

The Functionalist View in Accounting

The functionalist view in accounting focuses on explaining the social order, in which accounting plays a role, from a realist, positivist, determinist, and nomothetic standpoint. It is concerned with effective regulation on the basis of objective evidence.

The functionalist paradigm in accounting views accounting phenomena as concrete real-world relations possessing regularities and causal relationships that are amenable to scientific explanation and prediction.

In addition, the social order, as defined by extant structures of market and firm, is taken for granted, and no reference to domination or conflict is made. Both views of accounting phenomena and the social world are used to develop theories assumed to be value free rather than historically relative.

As in structural functionalism, the functionalist paradigm in accounting focuses on establishing the functions of accounting needed for an efficient operation of organizations. These functions are the "functional prerequisites" or "functional imperatives" of adaptation, goal attainment, integration, and latency or pattern maintenance. To serve these imperatives, the structures or elements of accounting are defined.

As in system theory, the functionalist paradigm in accounting focuses on both the search for analogical representation of the accounting system and a system analysis.

Interactionism with its focus on human association and interaction is expressed in the form of behavioral accounting.

Objectivism with its commitment to the models and methods used in the natural sciences is the predominant avenue in accounting theorizing and research. In fact, abstract empiricism as a label fits perfectly most of the published empirical accounting research. There is a definite urge to develop rigorous models of the accounting phenomena in the absence of confounding variables and a methodological reliance on hypothetic-deductive methods.

The functionalist view in accounting characterizes what is generally considered as mainstream accounting research. Its dominant assumptions include the following: "Theory is separate from observations that may be used to verify or falsify a theory. Hypothetic-deductive account of scientific explanation accepted. Quantitative methods of data analysis and collection which allows generalization favored."[15]

The Interpretive View in Accounting

The interpretive view in accounting would focus on explaining the social order from a nominalist, antipositivist, voluntarist, and ideological standpoint. If it existed in accounting it would aim to understand the subjective experience of individuals involved in the preparation, communication, verification, or use of accounting information. Hermeneutics, if applied in accounting, would focus on the study of the accounting objectification, like accounting institutions, accounting texts, accounting literature, accounting languages, and accounting ideologies, using the method of *verstehen*.

Phenomenology, if applied to accounting, would attempt to make explicit the "essences" that cannot be revealed by ordinary positivist observations. The interpretive paradigm in accounting, although in its infancy, has focused on (1) the ability of information to "construct reality,"[16] (2) the role of accounting as a "linguistic" tool,[17] and (3) other roles and images that accounting may take.[18]

To the interpretists, accounting is no more than names, concepts, and labels used to construct social reality. It can be understood only from the point of view of those directly involved in its preparation, communication, or use. Methodologically, ideographic methods rather than hypothetic-deductive methods are needed to reenact the actor's definition of the problem.

Therefore the dominant assumptions of the interpretive view in accounting should be:

A. Beliefs About Knowledge
Scientific explanations of human intention sought. Their adequacy is assessed via the criteria of logical consistency, subjective interpretation, and agreements with actors' common-sense interpretation.

B. Beliefs About Physical and Social Reality
Social reality is emergent, subjectively created, and objectified through human interaction. All actions have meaning and intention that are retrospectively endowed and that are grounded in social and historical practices. Social order is assumed. Conflict mediated through common schemes of social meanings.

C. Relationship Between Theory and Practice
Theory seeks to explain action and to understand how social order is produced and reproduced.[19]

Although the interpretive paradigm is not predominant in accounting, it suffers from three major limitations: (1) it assumes that a "quasi-divine" observer can understand social action through sheer subjectivity and without interference; (2) it creates the illusion of pure theory by using a monological line of reasoning; and (3) it fails to be an inquiry of change.[20]

The Radical Humanist View in Accounting

The radical humanist view in accounting would focus on explaining the social order from a nominalist, antipositivist, voluntarist, and ideographic perspective and places emphasis on forms of radical change. It respects any research that reduces philosophical critique to some normative methodology. In the form of critical theory it requires two forms of analysis: "(a) a taxonomic analysis of the ontological, epistemological, and methodological concerns underlying organization science; and (b) a critique (based on this analysis) of the dynamic interplay between organizational research, theory and practice."[21] It will expand its epistemic critique to include: "(a) a discussion of the limitation of alternative modes of inquiry; (b) an analysis of the relationship between the community of organizational researchers and organizational practitioners and members; and (c) the acknowledgment of the practical aim of any particular mode of research."[22]

Critical theory in accounting will assume that theories, bodies of knowledge, and facts are mere reflections of a realistic worldview. It will view accountants, accountors, and accountees as prisoners of a mode of consciousness that is shaped and controlled through ideological processes. All aspects of accounting will be scrutinized for their alienating properties. In short, accounting will be viewed as creating a "psychic prison" where organizational realities become confirming and dominating. The argument is that accounting systems encourage and sustain alienation and conflict. This view would suggest that accounting should help people realize their potential by helping them realize their needs, or would direct it to avenues in line with Habermas' concern with communicative competence and Gramsci's and Lukacs' concern with ideology and false consciousness.[23]

Gramsci, in particular, addressed the problem of false consciousness by examining the position of intellectuals in comtemporary society. Although he argued that all humans are intellectual beings, not everyone under capitalism performs intellectual functions. He further distinguished between traditional intellectuals, who historically have been autonomous of class interests, and organic intellectuals, who are ideologically aligned with class interests. In contemporary capitalism most intellectuals are organically tied to the bourgeoisie. Because of the ideological hegemony of capitalism, few intellectuals articulate the interests of the subordinate class. This type of radical humanist interpretation applied to the field of accounting suggests that until an "organic" elite of accountants emerge who are not tied ideologically to the capitalist class, the discipline of accounting will continue to reproduce the interests and the ideology of capitalism. Classical or functionalist accountants, however, will be very quick to accuse the humanist of being partisan and nonacademic. As Burrell and Morgan discussed, humanists are often labeled as "radicals hellbent upon fanning the flames of revolutionary consciousness, or as mindless existentialists who will not or cannot adjust to the world of everyday 'reality' and accept the inevitable march of 'progress.' "[24]

The Radical Structuralist View in Accounting

The radical structuralist view in accounting would challenge the social order from a realist, positivist, deterministic, and nomothetic standpoint. It would seek radical change, emancipation, and potentiality using an analysis emphasizing structural conflict, modes of domination, contradiction, and deprivation. This paradigm would generate accounting theories based upon metaphors such as the instrument of domination, schismatic system, and catastrophe.

The role of accounting in Weber's classic analysis of bureaucracy as a mode of domination, in Robert Michels' analysis of the "iron law of oligarchy," and in Marxists' analyses of organization will emerge as a powerful instrument of domination to be understood as an essential part of a wider process of domination within society as a whole. As stated by David Cooper,

From the point of view of these radical structuralists, organizations are instruments of social forces concerned to maintain the division of labour and distribution of wealth and power in society. To these researchers, whose perspective seems almost completely missing in current accounting research, there is an actuality of organization that includes sexual and racial discrimination, patterns of social stratification and unequal distributions of wealth, power and rewards. . . . The failure to acknowledge these characteristics and consider the relationship of accounting practices to them seems a curious omission for studies that explicitly seek to account for accounting.[25]

Structuralist accountants will hold an objective view of the social world but focus on contradictions and crisis tendencies created by the accounting process. Unlike the radical humanists with their emphasis on superstructural phenomena such as ideology and distorted consciousness, the radical structuralists in accounting will focus on the link between accounting and the economic and political relations of domination.

Marxist structuralists such as Althusser and Nicos Poulantzas have stressed the relative autonomy of political and ideological structures from the underlying economic base as a connective to the overly deterministic models of classical Marxists. With respect to the accounting enterprise, this approach would focus on the relative independence of accounting practices, policies, and theories from overt, economic, and political forces. The development of accounting could be seen as a *sui generis* process, defined from within. A similar agenda for accounting within the radical structuralist school has been eloquently stated as follows:

Radical theories may also be applied to more specific accounting questions: What underlies major shifts in the regulatory practices of the state and how much importance should accountants attribute to these changes? What determines the state's level of autonomy vis-à-vis advantaged and disadvantaged groups and, in this regard, how much credence may be attached to the view of writers, such as Benston, that disclosure regulations are captive of vested interest? Does the degree of state autonomy vary across regulatory spheres of interests? What stance should the accounting profession take in relation to the "contested terrain" of state regulation? Who are the sides in the struggle for control over the state's regulatory apparatus, and how should accountants choose a side to support? The continued dominance of neoclassical thought serves to exclude such questions from the accounting research agenda. This situation will persist as long as academic accounting falls short of the scholarly ideal that everything should be open for discussion in an intellectual community.[26]

CONCLUSIONS

Accounting theories and research are classified, following a framework introduced by Burrell and Morgan, into the functionalist, interpretive, radical humanist, and radical structuralist views. Each provides a unique approach for viewing and researching accounting phenomena. The relative merits of each view are not evaluated given the absence of a "paradigm neutral" metalanguage.[27] Each view, however, allows its proponents to have a unique understanding of the social order created by accounting as either displaying order or as divided by deep conflict and rests on assumptions of an ontological, epistemological, a methodological, and a human nature. Unlike another point of view, this pluralism of accounting views is satisfactory for a thorough disclosure of accounting theories or research.[28]

NOTES

1. Gibson Burrell and Gareth Morgan, *Sociological Paradigms and Organizational Analysis: Elements of the Sociology of Corporate Life* (London: Heinemann, 1979).

2. Ibid., p. 18.

3. Ibid., p. 22.

4. Ibid., p. xiii.

5. Ibid., p. 26.

6. Ibid., p. 88.

7. Ibid., p. 31.

8. W. Dilthey, *Selected Writings*, ed. H. P. Rickman (London: Cambridge University Press, 1976), p. 228.

9. H. G. Gadamer, *Wahrheit and Method* (Tubigen: J.C.B. Mohr; London: Sheed and Ward, 1975).

10. P. Thevenaz, *What Is Phenomenology?* (New York: Quadrangle, 1962), pp. 43–44.

11. Burrell and Morgan, *Sociological Paradigms and Organizational Analysis*, p. 248.

12. Ibid., p. 306.

13. Brian D. Steffy and Andrew J. Grimes, "A Critical Theory of Organizational Science," *Academy of Management Review* (April 1986), p. 323.

14. Ibid., p. 358.

15. Wai Fong, Chua, "Radical Development in Accounting Thought," *The Accounting Review* (October 1986), p. 611.

16. R. J. Boland, Jr. and L. R. Pondy, "Accounting in Organizations: A Union of Natural and Rational Perspectives," *Accounting, Organizations and Society* 5 (1980), pp. 223–34; S. Burchell et al., "The Roles of Accounting in Organizations and Society," *Accounting, Organizations and Society* 5 (1980), pp. 5–27; I. Colville, "Reconstructing 'Behavioral Accounting,' " *Accounting, Organizations and Society* 2/3 (1983), pp. 269–86; C. Tomkins and R. Groves, "The Everyday Accountant and Researching His Reality," *Accounting, Organizations and Society* 4 (1983), pp. 361–74.

17. Ahmed Belkaoui, "Linguistic Relativity in Accounting," *Accounting, Organizations and Society* (October 1978), pp. 97–194.

18. D. C. Hayes, "Accounting for Accounting: A Study about Managerial Accounting," *Accounting, Organizations and Society* 2/3 (1983), pp. 241–50.

19. Chua, "Radical Development in Accounting," p. 615.

20. Steffy and Grimes, "A Critical Theory of Organizational Science," p. 323.

21. Ibid., p. 324.

22. Ibid., p. 325.

23. J. Habermas, *Toward a Rational Society*, trans. J. J. Shapiro (Boston: Beacon Press, 1970); A. Gramsci, *Selections from the Prison Notebooks of Antonio Gramsci*, ed. Quinton Hoare and Geoffrey Nowell-Smith (London: Lawrence and Wishart, 1971); G. Lukacs, *History and Class Consciousness* (London: Merlin Press, 1973).

24. Burrell and Morgan, *Sociological Paradigms and Organizational Analysis*, p. 307.

25. David Cooper, "Tidiness, Muddle, and Things: Commonalities and Divergencies in Two Approaches to Management Accounting Research," *Accounting, Organizations and Society* 8 (1983), p. 277.

26. Anthony Tinker, "Theories of the State and the State of Accounting: Economic Reductionism and Political Voluntarism in Accounting Regulation Theory," *Journal of Accounting and Public Policy* (Spring 1984), p. 71.

27. T. S. Kuhn, *The Structure of Scientific Revolutions*, 2nd ed. (Chicago: University of Chicago Press, 1970).

28. A. M. Tinker, "Are Radical Humanists Really Libertarian Anarchists?" (Unpublished paper, 1984).

REFERENCES

Abdel-Khalik, A. R. and B. B. Ajinkya (1983). "An Evaluation of the Everyday Accountant and Researching His Reality." *Accounting, Organizations and Society* 4, pp. 375–84.

Althusser, L. (1971). *Lenin and Philosophy and Other Essays*. London: New Left Books.

Althusser, L. (1969). *For Marx*. Harmondsworth: Penguin.

Baran, P. and P. Sweezy. (1968). *Monopoly Capital*. Harmondsworth: Penguin.

Belkaoui, A. (1985). *Accounting Theory*, 2nd ed. New York: Harcourt Brace Jovanovich.

Belkaoui, A. (1980). *Conceptual Foundations of Management Accounting*. Reading, MA: Addison-Wesley.

Belkaoui, A. (October 1978). "Linguistic Relativity in Accounting." *Accounting, Organizations and Society*, pp. 97–104.

Belkaoui, A. (December 1984). "A Test of the Linguistic Relativity in Accounting." *Canadian Journal of Administrative Sciences*, pp. 238–55.

Benson, J. K. (1977). "Organizations: A Dialectical View." *Administrative Science Quarterly* 22, pp. 1–21.

Benson, J. K. (1977). "Paradigm and Praxis in Organizational Analysis." In L. L. Cummings and B. M. Staw, eds., *Research in Organizational Behavior*. New York: JAI Press, pp. 33–56.

Berkeley, G. (1962). *The Principles of Human Knowledge and Three Dialogs between Holas and Philonons*. London: Collins.

Bernstern, R. J. (1983). *Beyond Objectivism and Relativism: Science, Hermeneutics, and Praxis*. Philadelphia: University of Pennsylvania Press.

Blau, P. M. (1964). *Exchange and Power in Social Life*. New York: Wiley.

Bleicher, J. (1982). *The Hermeneutic Imagination*. Boston: Routledge & Kegan Paul.

Blumer, H. (1969). *Symbolic Interactionism: Perspective and Method*. Englewood Cliffs, NJ: Prentice-Hall.

Boland, R. J., Jr. and L. R. Pondy. (1980). "Accounting in Organizations: A Union of Natural and Rational Perspectives." *Accounting, Organizations and Society* 5, pp. 223–34.

Buckley, W. (1967). *Sociology and Modern Systems Theory*. Englewood Cliffs, NJ: Prentice-Hall.

Bukharin, N. (1965). *Historical Materialism: A System of Sociology*. New York: Russell and Russell.

Burchell, S. et al. (1980). "The Roles of Accounting in Organizations and Society." *Accounting, Organizations and Society* 5, pp. 5–27.

Burrell, Gibson and Gareth Morgan (1979). *Sociological Paradigms and Organizational Analysis: Elements of the Sociology of Corporate Life*. London: Heinemann.

Cherns, A. B. (1978). "Alienation and Accounting," *Accounting, Organizations and Society* 3, pp. 105–14.

Chua, W. F. (September 1984). "Diverse Perspectives in Management Accounting." Working Paper No. 13 (Sydney: University of Sydney, Accounting Research Centre).

Chua, W. F. et al. (December 1981). "Four Perspectives on Accounting Methodology." Paper presented at the Workshop on Accounting and Methodology, EIASM, Brussels.

Colletti, L. (1972). *From Rousseau to Lenin*. London: New Left Books.

Colville, I. (1983). "Reconstructing 'Behavioral Accounting.' " *Accounting, Organizations and Society* 2/3, pp. 269–86.

Comstock, D. E. and W. R. Scott (1983). "Technology and the Structure of Subunits: Distinguishing Individuals and Work-Group Effects." *Administrative Science Quarterly* 22, pp. 177–202.

Comte, Auguste (1853). *The Positivist Philosophy*, Vol. 1. London: Chapman.

Daft, R. L. and J. Wiginton (1979). "Language and Organization." *Academy of Management Review* 4, pp. 179–91.

Dallmayer, F. R. and T. A. McCarthy, eds. (1977). *Understanding and Social Inquiry*. Notre Dame, IN: University of Notre Dame Press.

Dilthey, W. (1976). *Selected Writings*, ed. H. P. Rickman. London: Cambridge University Press.

Douglas, J. D. (1970). *Understanding Everyday Life*. Chicago: Aldine; London: Routledge & Kegan Paul.

Dunlop, J. T. (1958). *Industrial Relations Systems*. New York: Holt, Rinehart and Winston.

Durkheim, E. (1953). *The Rules of Sociological Method*. Glencoe, IL: Free Press.

Easton, D. (1953). *The Political System*. New York: Knopf.

Evered, R. and M. R. Louis. (1981). "Alternative Perspective in the Organizational Sciences: 'Inquiry from the Inside and Inquiry from the Outside.' " *Academy of Management Review* 6, pp. 385–96.

Fischer, F. (1984). "Ideology and Organization Theory." In F. Fischer and C. Sirianni, eds., *Critical Studies in Organization and Bureaucracy*. Philadelphia: Temple University Press, pp. 135–71.

Frost, P. (1980). "Toward a Radical Framework for Practicing Organization Science." *Academy of Management Review* 5, pp. 501–8.

Gadamer, H. (1976). *Philosophical Hermeneutics*, trans. D. E. Linge. Berkeley: University of California Press.

Galtung, J. (1977). *Methodology and Ideology*. Copenhagen: Christian Ejlers.

Garfinkel, H. (1967). *Studies in Ethnomethodology*. Englewood Cliffs, NJ: Prentice-Hall, 1967.

Gergen, K. J. (1985). "The Social Constructionist Movement in Modern Psychology." *American Psychologist* 40, pp. 266–75.

Geuss, R. (1982). *The Idea of a Critical Theory*. London: Cambridge University Press.

Gramsci, A. (1971). *Selections from the Prison Notebooks of Antonio Gramsci*, ed. Quinton Hoare and Geoffrey Nowell-Smith. London: Lawrence and Wishart.

Granovetter, M. (1981). "Towards a Sociological Theory of Income Differences." In I. Berg, ed., *Sociological Perspectives on Labor Markets*. London: Academic Press, pp. 11–47.

Habermas, J. (1979). *Communication and the Evolution of Society*, trans. T. McCarthy. Boston: Beacon Press.

Habermas, J. (1971). *Knowledge and Human Interests*, trans. T. McCarthy. Boston: Beacon Press.

Habermas, J. (1973). *Knowledge and Practice*, trans. J. Viertel. Boston: Beacon Press.

Habermas, J. (1976). *Legitimation Crisis*, trans. T. McCarthy. Boston: Beacon Press, 1975; London: Heineman, 1976.

Habermas, J. (1970). *Toward a Rational Society*, trans. J. J. Shapiro. Boston: Beacon Press.

Habermas, J. (1970). "Towards a Theory of Communication Competence." *Inquiry* 13, pp. 360–75.

Hayes, D. C. (1983). "Accounting for Accounting: A Study about Managerial Accounting," *Accounting, Organizations and Society* 2/3, pp. 241–50.

Hayes, D. C. (1977). "The Contingency Theory of Managerial Accounting." *Accounting Review* 52, pp. 22–39.

Held, D. (1980). *Introduction to Critical Theory: Horkheimer to Habermas.* Berkeley: University of California Press.

Heydebrand, W. and B. Burris. (1984). "The Limits of Praxis in Critical Theory." In J. Marcus and Z. Tar, eds., *Foundations of the Frankfurt School of Social Research.* New Brunswick, NJ: Transaction Books, pp. 419–24.

Homans, G. C. (1950). *The Human Group.* New York: Harcourt Brace Jovanovich.

Hopper, T. and A. Powell. (November 1985). "Making Sense of Research into the Organizational and Social Aspects of Management Accounting: A Review of Its Underlying Assumptions." *Journal of Management Studies,* pp. 429–65.

Hopwood, A. G. (1983). "On Trying to Study Accounting in the Contexts in Which It Operates." *Accounting, Management Studies* 2/3, pp. 287–305.

Horkheimer, M. (1972). *Critical Theory: Selected Essays.* New York: Herder.

Howard, G. S. (1985). "The Role of Values in the Science of Psychology." *American Psychologist* 40, pp. 225–65.

Husserl, E. (1929). "Phenomenology." *Encyclopedia Britannica,* 14th ed.

Katouzian, H. (1980). *Ideology and Method in Economics.* London: Macmillan.

Katz, D. and R. L. Kahn. (1966). *The Social Psychology of Organizations.* New York: Wiley.

Kuhn, T. S. (1970). *The Structure of Scientific Revolution,* 2nd ed. Chicago: University of Chicago Press.

Laughlin, R. C. (December 1983). "The Need for and Nature of a Critical Theoretic Methodological Approach to the Design of Enterprise Accounting Systems." Paper presented to the workshop on Accounting and Methodology, EIASM, Brussels.

Lukacs, G. (1973). *History and Class Consciousness.* London: Merlin Press.

Lundberg, C. (1976). "Hypothesis Creation in Organizational Behavior Research." *Academy of Management Review* 1, pp. 5–12.

Luthans, F. and T. Davis. (1982). "An Ideographic Approach to Organizational Behavior Research: The Use of Single Case Experimental Designs and Direct Measures." *Academy of Management Review* 7, pp. 380–91.

Marcus, J. and Z. Tar. (1984). *Foundations of the Frankfurt School of Social Research.* New Brunswick, NJ: Transaction Books.

Marcuse, H. (1964). *One Dimensional Man.* London: Routledge & Kegan Paul.

Marques, E. (1976). "Human Resource Accounting: Some Questions and Reflections." *Accounting, Organizations and Society* 1, pp. 175–78.

Marx, K. (1976). *Capital: A Critique of Political Economy,* Vols 1–3, trans. B.

Fowkes. Harmondsworth: Penguin. Vol. 1 was first published in 1867; Vol. 2 in 1885; Vol. 3 in 1894.

McCarthy, T. (1978). *The Critical Theory of Jurgen Habermas*. Cambridge, MA: MIT Press.

Mead, G. H. (1934). *Mind, Self and Society*, ed. Charles Morris. Chicago: University of Chicago Press.

Merton, R. K. (1968). *Social Theory and Social Structure*. New York: Free Press.

Meyer, A. D. (1984). "Mingling Decision-Making Metaphors." *Academy of Management Review* 9, pp. 6–17.

Meyer, J. W. (1983). "On the Celebration of Rationality: Some Comments on Boland and Pondy." *Accounting, Organizations and Society* 2/3, pp. 235–40.

Miller, R. W. (1983). "Fact and Method in the Social Sciences." In D. R. Sabia and J. T. Wallulis, eds., *Critical Theory and Other Critical Perspectives*. Albany, NY: State University of New York, pp. 254–75.

Mitroff, I. I. and R. K. Kilman. (1978). *Methodological Approaches to Social Sciences*. San Francisco: Jossey-Bass.

Mitroff, I. I. and R. O. Mason. (1982). "Business Policy and Metaphysics: Some Philosophical Considerations." *Academy of Management Review* 7, pp. 361–70.

Morey, N. and F. Luthans. (1984). "An Emic Perspective and Ethnoscience Methods for Organizational Research." *Academy of Management Review* 9, pp. 27–36.

Morgan, G. (1983). "Social Science and Accounting Research: A Commentary on Tomkins and Groves." *Accounting, Organizations and Society* 4, pp. 385–88.

Morgan, G. and L. Smircich. (1980). "The Case for Qualitative Research." *Academy of Management Review* 5, pp. 491–500.

Natanson, M. (1966). *Essays in Phenomenology*. The Hague: Martinus Nijhoff.

Palmen, R. E. (1969). *Hermeneutics*. Evanston, IL: Northwestern University Press.

Pareto, V. (1935). *The Third Society*, 4 vols. New York: Harcourt Brace Jovanovich.

Parsons, T. (1951). *The Social System*. London: Tavistock; Glencoe, IL: Free Press.

Radcliffe-Brown, A. (1952). *Structure and Function in Primitive Society*. London: Cohen and West.

Ratcliffe, J. W. (1983). "Notions of Validity in Qualitative Research Methodology." *Knowledge* 2, pp. 147–67.

Sanday, P. R. (1979). "The Ethnographic Paradigm(s)." *Administrative Sciences Quarterly* 24, pp. 527–38.

Sanders, P. (1982). "Phenomenology: A New Way of Viewing Organizational Research." *Academy of Management Review* 7, pp. 353–60.

Sartre, J. (1966). *Being and Nothingness*. New York: Washington Square Press.

Sartre, J. (1976). *Critique of Dialectical Reason*, trans. A. Sheridan-Smith. London: Verso.

Schroyer, T. (1973). *Critique of Domination*. New York: George Braziller.

Schutz, A. and T. Luckmann (1974). *The Structures of the Life World*. London: Heineman.

Shrivastava, P. and I. Mitroff. (1984). "Enhancing Organizational Research Utilization: The Role of Decision Makers' Assumptions." *Academy of Management Review* 9, pp. 18–26.

Simmel, G. (1955). *Conflict and the Web of Group Affiliation*. Glencoe, IL: Free Press.

Skinner, B. F. (1978). *Beyond Freedom and Dignity*. New York: Knopf.

Spencer, H. (1973). *The Study of Sociology*. London: Kegan Paul and Tench.

Steffy, Brian D. and Andrew J. Grimes. (April 1986). "A Critical Theory of Organizational Science." *Academy of Management Review*, pp. 322–36.

Thomas, K. W. and W. G. Tymon. (1982). "Necessary Properties of Relevant Research: Lessons from Recent Criticism of the Organizational Sciences." *Academy of Management Review* 7, pp. 345–52.

Tinker, A. M. (1984). "Are Radical Humanists Really Libertarian Anarchists?" (Unpublished paper).

Tinker, A. M. (July 1983). "The Naturalization of Accounting: Social Ideology and the Genesis of Agency Theory." Working Paper, New York University.

Tinker, A. M. (Spring 1984). "Theories of the State and the State of Accounting: Economic Reductionism and Political Voluntarism in Accounting Regulation Theory." *Journal of Accounting and Public Policy*, pp. 55–74.

Tinker, A. M. (1980). "Towards a Political Economy of Accounting: An Empirical Illustration of the Cambridge Controversies." *Accounting, Organizations and Society* 5, pp. 147–60.

Tinker, A. M., B. D. Merino, and M. D. Neimark. (1982). "The Normative Origins of Positive Theories: Ideology and Accounting Thought." *Accounting, Organizations and Society* 7, pp. 167–200.

Tinker, A. M. and M. D. Neimark. (July 1983). "Historical Accounting Research as an Emancipatory Practice: Restoring Our Collective Memory Using Annual Reports." Working Paper, New York University.

Tomkins, C. and R. Groves. (1983). "The Everyday Accountant and Researching His Reality." *Accounting, Organizations and Society* 4, pp. 407–18.

Turner, R. ed. (1974). *Ethnomethodology*. Harmondsworth: Penguin.

Van Maanen, J. (1979). "Reclaiming Qualitative Methods for Organizational Research: A Preface." *Administrative Science Quarterly* 4, pp. 520–26.

Von Bertalanffy, L. (1956). "General Systems Theory." *General Systems* 1, pp. 1–10.

Warren, S. (1984). *The Emergence of Dialectical Theory*. Chicago: University of Chicago Press.

Weber, M. (1949). *The Methodology of the Social Sciences*, trans. E. Shils and H. Finch. New York: Free Press.

Weber, M. (1947). *The Theory of Social and Economic Organization*. Glencoe, IL: Free Press.

Willmott, H. C. (1983). "Paradigms for Accounting Research: Critical Reflections on Tomkins and Groves." *Accounting, Organizations and Society* 4, pp. 389–406.

3
PERSPECTIVES ON ACCOUNTING PARADIGMS

Not long ago, a contempt for accounting existed within and without the university. In an address to the American Association of University Instructors in Accounting on December 29, 1923, Henry Rand Hatfield described the situation as follows:

I am sure that all of us who teach accounting in the universities suffer from the implied contempt of our colleagues, who look upon accounting as an intruder, a Saul among the prophets, a pariah whose very presence detracts somewhat from the sanctity of the academic halls. It is true that we ourselves speak of the science of accounts, or of the art of accounting, even of the philosophy of accounts. But accounting, is alas, only a pseudo-science unrecognized by J. McKeen Cattel: its products are displayed neither in the salon nor in the national academy; one finds it discussed by neither realist, idealist nor phenomenalist. The humanists look down upon us as beings who dabble in the sordid figures of dollars and cents instead of toying with infinities and searching for the elusive soul of things, the scientists and technologists despise us as able only to record rather than to perform deeds.[1]

Fortunately the situation has changed dramatically. The quantity and quality of research findings in accounting are evidence of the academic status of accounting.

There is a lot of tension in accounting research due to the presence of competing paradigms, each of which is striving for supremacy. Journals and research centers are created, and workshops, conferences, and round-tables are used to give credibility to each paradigm. It is a normal situation

observable in every other field. Each of these paradigms is the object of investigation and research by established scientific communities. In each of
these communities, a paradigm creates a coherent, united viewpoint—a
kind of *Weltanschauung*—that determines the way in which members
view accounting research, practice, and even education. In the interests of
continuity and progress within the accounting discipline, these paradigms
are subjected to constant verification and testing in the search for possible
anomalies. Accordingly, this chapter attempts to explicate the different visions in accounting paradigms.

REVOLUTIONARY CHANGES, THEORIES, AND THE PUNCTUATED EQUILIBRIUM PARADIGM

How do disciplines change? The question has been debated for a long
time. Darwinism with its notion of incremental, cumulative change is far
from being adequate for explaining changes in disciplines and growth of
knowledge. Instead natural historians like Niles Eldredge and Stephen
Gould[2] propose a different notion of evolution known as punctuated
equilibrium: an alternative between long periods with stable infrastruc-
tures and incremental adaptation and brief periods of revolutionary
upheaval. Basically, "lineages exist in essentially static form (equilibrium) over most of their histories and new species arise abruptly, through
sudden, revolutionary 'punctuations' of rapid change (at which point—
as in the Darwinian model—environmental selection determines the fate
of new variations)."[3] As Exhibit 3.1 shows, the punctuated equilibrium
model has been described in six theories, including individuals, groups,
organizations, scientific fields, biological species, and grand theory. Exhibit 3.2 shows how punctuated equilibrium models differ from traditional counterparts. For each theory the punctuated equilibrium offers
three main components: deep structure, equilibrium periods, and revolutionary periods. The interest in this chapter is with the application of
the punctuated equilibrium paradigm to scientific fields in general and
accounting in particular.

KUHN'S GENERAL THEORY OF SCIENTIFIC REVOLUTIONS

A theory of scientific revolutions will focus on the progress of knowledge and the motivation of such progress. Thomas Kuhn's works focused
on the progress of knowledge in a particular discipline of normal sci-

Exhibit 3.1
Concepts of Equilibrium Periods in Six Theories

Concepts of Equilibrium Periods in Six Theories

Commonalities:
During equilibrium periods, systems maintain and carry out the choices of their deep structure. Systems make adjustments that preserve the deep structure against internal and external perturbations, and move incrementally along paths built into the deep structure. Pursuit of stable deep structure choices may result in behavior that is turbulent on the surface.

Individuals: Levinson
  Structure-Building Periods: The primary task is to build a life structure: a man must make certain key choices, form a structure around them, and pursue his goals and values within this structure. To say that a period is stable in this sense is not . . . to say that it is tranquil. . . . The task of . . . building a structure is often stressful . . . and may involve many kinds of change. Each stable period . . . has distinctive tasks and character according to where it is in the life cycle. (1978: 49) [Such periods] ordinarily last 5 to 7 years, 10 at most. (1986: 7)

Groups: Gersick (1988)
  Project groups' lives unfold in two main Phases, separated by a transition period halfway between the group's beginning and its expected deadline. Within phases, groups approach their work using stable frameworks of assumptions, premises, and behavior patterns. As frameworks vary, specific activities and efficacy vary from group to group. During a phase, groups accumulate more or less work, learning, and experience within the boundaries of their framework, but (even when hampered by it), they do not change their fundamental approach to their task.

Organizations: Tushman & Romanelli (1985)
  Convergent Periods: Relatively long time spans of incremental change and adaptation which elaborate structure, systems, controls, and resources toward increased coalignment, [which] may or may not be associated with effective performance. (: 173) [They are] characterized by duration, strategic orientation, [and] turbulence. . . . (: 179) During [these] periods . . . inertia increases and competitive vigilance decreases; structure frequently drives strategy. (: 215)

Scientific Fields: Kuhn (1970)
  Normal Science is directed to the articulation of those phenomena and theories that the paradigm already supplies. (: 24) Three classes of problems—determination of significant fact, matching of facts with theory, and articulation of theory—exhaust . . . the literature of normal science, both empirical and theoretical. . . . Work under that paradigm can be conducted in no other way, and to desert the paradigm is to cease practicing the science it defines. (: 34)

Biological Species: Gould (1980)
  Phyletic transformation [is] minor adjustment within populations [which is] sequential and adaptive. (: 15) [It is a mode of evolution in which] an entire population changes from one state to another. [This] yields no increase in diversity, only a transformation of one thing into another. Since extinction (by extirpation, not by evolution into something else) is so common, a biota with [only this, and] no mechanism for increasing diversity would soon be wiped out. (: 180)

Grand Theory: Prigogine & Stengers (1984); Haken (1981)
  In stable regions, deterministic laws dominate. (: 169) All individual initiative is doomed to insignificance. . . . (: 206)
  Under given external conditions, the individual parts of the system have . . . stable configurations . . . or oscillations. . . . [If] small perturbations [are] imposed upon the system . . . the individual parts of the system relax to their former state once the perturbation is removed, or they change their behavior only slightly when the perturbation persists. (: 17)

Source: Connie J. G. Gersick, "Revolutionary Change Theories: A Multilevel Exploration of the Punctuated Equilibrium Paradigm," *Academy of Management Review* 16, no. 1 (1991), p. 13. Reprinted with permission.

Exhibit 3.2
Concepts of Deep Structure in Six Theories

Concepts of Deep Structure in Six Theories

Commonalities:

Deep structure is a network of fundamental, interdependent "choices," of the basic configuration into which a system's units are organized, and the activities that maintain both this configuration and the system's resource exchange with the environment. Deep structure in human systems is largely implicit.

Individuals: Levinson (1986: 6)

Life Structure: The underlying pattern or design of a person's life at a given time. . . . The life structure [answers the questions]: "What is my life like now? What are the most important parts of my life, and how are they interrelated? Where do I invest most of my time and energy?" The primary components of a life structure are the person's relationships with various others in the external world.

Groups: Gersick (see 1988: 17, 21)

Framework: A set of givens about the group's situation and how it will behave that form a stable platform from which the group operates. Frameworks may be partly explicit but are primarily implicit. They are integrated webs of performance strategies, interaction patterns, assumptions about and approaches toward a group's task and outside context.

Organizations: Tushman & Romanelli (1985: 176)

Strategic Orientation: Answers the question: What is it that is being converged upon? While [it] may or may not be explicit, it can be described by [five facets]: (1) core beliefs and values regarding the organization, its employees and its environment; (2) products, markets, technology and competitive timing; (3) the distribution of power; (4) the organization's structure; and (5) the nature, type and pervasiveness of control systems.

Scientific Fields: Kuhn (1970)

Paradigm: Universally recognized scientific achievements that for a time provide model problems and solutions to a community of practitioners. (: viii) [Paradigms indicate] what a datum [is], what instruments might be used to retrieve it, and what concepts [are] relevant to its interpretation. (: 122) [However, scientists] are little better than laymen at characterizing the established bases of their field. . . . Such abstractions show mainly through their ability to do successful research. (: 47)

Biological Species. Gould (1989); Wake, Roth, & Wake (1983: 218–219)*

Genetic Programs: Stasis is . . . an active feature of organisms and populations . . . based largely on complex epistasis in genetic programs, and the resilient and limited geometries of developmental sequences. (: 124)

[Living systems require very specific internal processes.] The . . . conditions governing each internal process are provided by preceding processes within the system, [constituting a network of] circular interaction: [the activity of each element affects all]. Each . . . change of the system must remain within the . . . limits of the process of circular production and maintenance of the elements, or the system itself will decompose. No element can interact with the environment independently . . . and no independent change (evolution) of single elements can take place. . . . The same is true for the "activity" of the genes: they never "express" themselves in a direct, linear way. Thus organisms have evolved as systems resistant to change, even genetic change.

Grand Theory: Haken (1981: 17)

Order Parameters: Collective modes . . . which define the order of the overall system. . . . Order parameters . . . may be material, such as the amplitude of a physical wave, [or] immaterial, such as ideas or symbols. . . . Once . . . established, they prescribe the actions of the subsystems . . . at the microscopic level.

* The Wake et al. excerpt is from an article recommended by S. J. Gould (personal communication). It explains and expands on the excerpt from Gould.

Source: Connie J. G. Gersick, "Revolutionary Change Theories: A Multilevel Exploration of the Punctuated Equilibrium Paradigm," *Academy of Management Review* 16, no. 1 (1991), p. 14. Reprinted with permission.

ence.[4] This thesis of scientific revolutions rests on the concept of paradigm. After criticisms were raised about the different and inconsistent uses of the term, Kuhn refined it for the second editions of his book:

In much of the book the term "paradigm" is used in two different senses. On the one hand, it stands for the entire constellation of beliefs, values, techniques that are shared by the members of a given community. On the other hand it denotes one sort of element in that constellation, the concrete puzzle-solutions which, employed as models or examples, can replace explicit rules as a basis for the solution of the remaining puzzles of normal science.[5]

These paradigms do not remain forever dominant. Anomalies are first recognized. The anomaly is incorrigible. A period of insecurity and crisis arises with a dispute between those who see the anomaly as a counter-example and those who do not: "Normal science repeatedly goes astray. And when it does—when, that is, the profession can no longer evade anomalies that subvert the existing tradition of scientific practice—then begins the extraordinary investigation that leads the profession at last to a new set of commitments, a new basis for the practice of science."[6]

The crisis continues with the emergence of alternative sets of ideas and clear identification of schools of thoughts. What actually goes on in the crisis period is not well known. H. Gilman McCann suggested the following characteristic levels of theoretical and quantitative work associated with the initial and final periods of a normal science.

1. The level of theoretical work will rise as the revolution develops. The rise is composed of (a) an increase in the level of theoretical work among followers of the given paradigm and (b) an initially high level of theoretical work by the followers of the new paradigm, followed by a decline once the success of the new paradigm is assured.

2. The shift to the new paradigm will occur earlier among theoretical papers than among others.

3. The level of quantitative work will rise as the revolution develops. The rise is composed of (a) an increase, possibly followed by a decline, in the level of work among the followers of the given paradigm and (b) an initially high level of quantitative work among supporters of the new paradigm, possibly followed by a decline as the new paradigm succeeds and new problems come to light.

4. The shift to the new paradigm will occur earlier among quantitative papers than among others.

5. The rise in the level of quantitative work will be most pronounced among theoretical papers.

6. There will be an increase in the number of authors as the revolution develops.

7. There will be an increase in the productivity of authors as the revolution progresses.

8. The shift to the new paradigm will occur earlier among papers of younger authors than among papers of older ones.

9. The supporters of the new paradigm will be younger than the defenders of the old one.

10. There will be few neutral papers.

11. The proportion of citations to authors supporting the new paradigm will increase during the revolution.[7]

All laws and propositions become subject to empirical testimony. The final rejection of one paradigm for another does not, however, rest exclusively on empirical evidence. Nonlogical factors, including metaphysical views, philosophical positions, ethnocentrism, nationalism, and the social characteristics of the scientific community, may have a bearing on the decision.[8] Domination of the new paradigm is accompanied by recognition bestowed on its proponents. It is this recognition, rather than money or power, which will become the motivating factor for researchers in a given paradigm and in a given scientific community. Basically, researchers will exchange social recognition for information. As stated by W. O. Hagstrom: "Manuscripts submitted to scientific periodicals are often called "contributions," and they are, in fact, gifts."[9]

In general, the acceptance of a gift by an individual or a community implies a kind of recognition of the status of the donor and the existence of certain kinds of reciprocal rights. . . . in science, the acceptance by scientific journals of contributed manuscripts establishes the donor's status as a scientist—indeed, status as a scientist can be achieved only by much gift-giving—and it assures him of prestige within the scientific community.[10]

Although it may be difficult to disagree with the notion that recognition is the primary motivation for research in any discipline, it is tempting to argue that the driving force is the satisfaction of a job well done. R. K. Merton argued the case as follows:

Recognition of originality becomes socially validated testimony that one has successfully lived up to the most exacting requirements of one's role as a scientist. The self-image of the individual scientist will also depend greatly on the appraisals by his scientific peers of the extent to which he has lived up to this exacting and crucially important aspect of his role.[11]

There is, nevertheless, a gem of psychological truth in the suspicion enveloping the drive for recognition in science. Any intrinsic reward—game, money, position—is morally ambiguous and potentially subversive of culturally esteemed values. For as rewards are meted out, they can displace the original motive: concern with recognition can displace concern with advancing knowledge.[12]

With recognition as either a goal or a sign of a job well done, the researchers in the dominant paradigm, and the other still struggling paradigms ("the resisters"), communicate their information either in formal channels of communication for institutional recognition or indirect communication for elementary recognition.

RITZER'S VISIONS OF MULTIPLE PARADIGM APPLIED TO ACCOUNTING

Central to the general theory of scientific revolutions is the proper definition of the concept of a paradigm. Kuhn's use of the term is different and inconsistent. The narrow definition provided in the epilogue to the second edition of his book was still found vague. It did not alleviate the major criticisms directed toward Kuhn's change of view that paradigms rise and fall as a result of political factors to the view that one paradigm wins over another for good reasons, including "accuracy, scope, simplicity, fruitfulness, and the like."[13] George Ritzer, for example, argued in favor of the first view and maintained that the emergence of a paradigm is essentially a political phenomenon.[14] He stated:

One paradigm wins out over another because its supporters have more *power* than those who support competing paradigms and *not* necessarily because their paradigm is "better" than its competitors. For example, the paradigm whose supporters control the most important journals in a field and thereby determine what will be published is more likely to gain pre-eminence than paradigms whose adherents lack access to prestigious outlets for their works. Similarly, positions of leadership in a field are likely to be given to supporters of the dominant paradigm and this gives them a platform to enunciate their position with a significant amount of legitimacy. Supporters of paradigms that are seeking to gain hegemony within a field are obviously at a disadvantage, since they lack the power outlined above. Nevertheless, they can, by waging a political battle of their own, overthrow a dominant paradigm and gain that position for themselves.[15]

A. Phillips was in agreement with Ritzer's arguments about the first view and also argued that the reasons advanced in the second view are paradigm-dependent.

With the view that paradigms are politics-dependent, Ritzer offered the following definition of a paradigm:

A paradigm is a fundamental image of the subject matter within a science. It serves to define what should be studied, what questions should be asked, how they should be asked, and what rules should be followed in interpreting the answer obtained. The paradigm is the broadest unit of consensus within a science and serves to differentiate one scientific community (or subcommunity) from another. It subsumes, defines, and interrelates the exemplars, theories, methods, and instruments that exist within it.[16]

The basic components of a paradigm emerge from Ritzer's definition: (1) an *exemplar*, or a piece of work that stands as a model for those who work within the paradigm; (2) an *image* of the subject matter; (3) *theories*; and (4) *methods* and instruments.

This chapter uses Ritzer's definition to analyze scientific communities or subcommunities in accounting with the assumptions that (1) accounting lacks a single comprehensive paradigm and is a multiple-paradigm science, and (2) each of these accounting paradigms is striving for acceptance, even domination within the discipline. Although stated in terms of competing theories, the following statement could be used to argue for competing paradigms:

While the value of the prediction of a theory to users influences its use, it does not solely determine its success. Because the costs of errors and the implementation vary, several theories about the phenomena can exist simultaneously for predictive purposes. However, only one will be generally accepted by theorists. In accepting one theory over another, theorists will be influenced by the intuitive appeal of the theory's explanation for phenomena and the range of phenomena it can explain and predicts as well as by the usefulness of its predictions to users.[17]

Following suggestions made by the 1977 American Accounting Association's publication of its *Statement of Accounting Theory and Theory Acceptance*, the following paradigms were suggested:[18]

1. The anthropological/inductive paradigm
2. The true-income/deductive paradigm
3. The decision-usefulness/decision-model paradigm
4. The decision-usefulness/decision-maker/aggregate-market-behavior paradigm
5. The decision-usefulness/decision-maker/individual-user paradigm
6. The information/economics paradigm

Paradigms 1–5 are examined next with a particular focus on the four components of exemplar, image, theories, and methods.

THE ANTHROPOLOGICAL/INDUCTIVE PARADIGM

Exemplar

R. R. Sterling characterized what he called "the anthropological interpretation of accounting" as probably the most ancient and pervasive method of accounting theory construction, and its method is to "observe accountants' actions and then rationalize these actions by subsuming them under generalized principles."[19] Examples include the works of S. Gilman, H. R. Hatfield, W. A. Paton, A. C. Littleton, and Y. Ijiri.[20]

Other studies by M. J. Gordon and by R. L. Watts and J. L. Zimmerman qualify as examples of the anthropological/inductive paradigm.[21] Both studies argue that management will select the accounting rule that tend to smooth income and the rate of growth in income.[22]

Several empirical tests in the income-smoothing literature leave Gordon's model unconfirmed. Also, Gordon's assumptions that shareholder satisfaction is solely a positive function of income and that increases in stock prices always follow increases in accounting income have been seriously contested. To avoid the pitfalls that may exist in Gordon's model, Watts and Zimmerman attempted to provide a positive theory of accounting by exploring the factors influencing management's attitudes regarding accounting standards.[23] At the outset, Watts and Zimmerman assumed that management's utility is a positive function of the expected compensation in future periods and a negative function of the dispersions of future compensation. Their analysis showed that the choice of accounting standards can affect a firm's cash flow through taxes, regulation, political costs, information production costs, and management-compensation plans.

Image of the Subject Matter

To those who adopt the anthropological/inductive paradigm, the basic subject matter is (1) existing accounting practices and (2) management's attitudes toward those practices. Proponents of this view argue in general either that the techniques are derived and justified on the basis of their tested use or that management plays a central role in determining the techniques to be implemented. Consequently, the accounting-research objective associated with the anthropological/inductive paradigm is to understand, explain, and predict existing accounting practices.

Theories

Four theories may be considered to be part of the anthropological/inductive paradigm: (1) information economics,[24] (2) the analytical/agency model,[25] (3) the income smoothing/earnings management hypotheses,[26] and (4) the positive theory of accounting.[27]

Methods

Those who adopt the anthropological/inductive paradigm tend to employ one of three techniques: (1) techniques used in income smoothing research,[28] (2) techniques used in earnings management research,[29] and (3) techniques used in positive theory research.[30]

THE TRUE-INCOME/DEDUCTIVE PARADIGM

Exemplars

Studies that qualify as exemplars of the true-income/deductive paradigm are the works of W. A. Paton, J. B. Canning, Henry Sweeney, Kenneth MacNeal, Sidney Alexander, E. O. Edwards & P. W. Bell, Maurice Moonitz, and R. T. Sprouse & Maurice Moonitz.[31] These authors share a concern for a normative-deductive approach to the construction of an accounting theory and, with the exception of Alexander, a belief that, ideally, income measured using a single valuation base would meet the needs of all users. These researchers are also in complete agreement that current price information is more useful than conventional historical-cost information to users in making economic decisions.

Image of the Subject Matter

To those who adopt the true-income/deductive paradigm, the basic subject matter is (1) the construction of an accounting theory on the basis of logical and normative reasoning and conceptual rigor, and (2) a concept of ideal income based on some method other than the historical-cost method. MacNeal argued for an ideal-income concept as follows: "there is one correct definition of profits in an accounting sense. A 'profit' is an increase in net wealth. A 'loss' is a decrease in net wealth. This is an economist's definition. It is terse, obvious, and mathematically demonstrable."[32] Alexander, who also argued for an ideal-income concept, states: "We must find out whether economic income is an ideal from which accounting differs only to the degree that the ideal is practically unattainable, or whether economic income is inappropriate even if it could conveniently be measured."[33]

Theories

The theories that emerge from the true-income/deductive paradigm present alternatives to the historical-cost accounting system. In general, five theories or schools of thought may be identified: (1) price-level-adjusted (or current-purchasing power) accounting,[34] (2) replacement-cost accounting,[35] (3) deprival-value accounting,[36] (4) continuously contemporary (net-realizable-value) accounting,[37] and (5) present-value accounting.[38] Each of these theories presents alternative methods of asset valuation and income determination that allegedly overcome the defect of the historical-cost accounting system.

Methods

Those who accept the true-income/deductive paradigm generally employ analytic reasoning to justify the construction of an accounting theory or to argue the advantages of a particular asset-valuation/income-determination model other than historical-cost accounting. Advocates of this paradigm generally proceed from objectives and postulates about the environment to specific methods.

THE DECISION-USEFULNESS/DECISION-MODEL PARADIGM

Exemplars

The works of W. H. Beaver, J. W. Kennelly, and W. M. Voss and of Robert Sterling may be considered the true exemplars of the decision-usefulness/decision-model paradigm.[39] Beaver, Kennelly, and Voss examined the origin of the predictive-ability criterion, its relationship to the facilitation of decision making, and the potential difficulties associated with its implementation. According to the predictive-ability criterion, alternative methods of accounting measurement are evaluated in terms of their ability to predict economic events.

The predictive-ability criterion is presented as a purposive criterion in that accounting data ought to be evaluated in terms of their purpose or use, which is generally accepted in accounting to be the facilitation of decision making. The predictive-ability criterion is assumed to be relevant, even when applied in conjunction with a low specification of the decision model.

Sterling developed criteria to be used in evaluating the various measures of wealth and income. Given the conflicting viewpoints about the objectives of accounting reports, Sterling chose usefulness as the overriding criterion of a measurement method, emphasizing its importance over requirements such as objectivity and verifiability.[40]

Due to the diversity of decision makers and the inherent economic and physical impossibility of providing all of the information that users want, Sterling opted for usefulness as the relevant criterion of decision models:

The basis for selection that I prefer is to supply information for rational decision models. The modifier "rational" is defined to mean those decision models that are most likely to allow decision makers to achieve their goals.[41] . . . In summary, an accounting system should be designed to provide relevant information to rational decision models. The accounting system cannot supply all the information desired by all decision makers and, therefore, we must decide to exclude some kinds of information and to include other kinds. Restricting the decision models to rational ones permits the exclusion of a raft of data based on the whims of decision makers. It permits us to concentrate on those models that have been demonstrated to be effective in achieving the decision makers' goal.[42]

Image of the Subject Matter

To those who adopt the decision-usefulness/decision-model paradigm, the basic subject matter is the usefulness of accounting information to decision models. Information relevant to a decision model or criterion is determined and then implemented by choosing the best accounting alternative. Usefulness to a decision model is equated with relevance to a decision model.

Theories

Two kinds of theories may be included within the decision usefulness/decision-model paradigm. The first type of theory deals with the different kinds of decision models associated with business decision making: EOQ, PERT, linear-programming, capital budgeting, buy versus lease, make or buy, and so on. The information requirements for most of these decision models are fairly well specified. The second kind of theory deals with the different economic events that may affect a going concern (bankruptcy, takeover, merger, bond ratings, and so on). Theories to link accounting information to these events are still lacking. Developing such theories is the primary objective of those working within the decision-usefulness/decision-making model paradigm.

Methods

Those who accept the decision-usefulness/decision-model paradigm tend to rely on empirical techniques to determine the predictive ability of selected items of information. The general approach has been to use discriminant analysis to classify firms into one of several a priori groupings, dependent on a firm's individual financial characteristics.

THE DECISION-USEFULNESS/DECISION-MAKER/ AGGREGATE-MARKET-BEHAVIOR PARADIGM

Exemplars

The exemplars of the decision-usefulness/decision-maker/aggregate-market-behavior paradigm are the works of N. J. Gonedes and of Gonedes and Nicholas Dopuch.[43] In his pioneering paper, Gonedes extended the interest in decision usefulness from the individual-user response to the aggregate-market response. Arguing that market responses (for example, anticipatory price responses) to accounting numbers should govern the evaluation of the informational content of these numbers and of the procedures used to produce them, Gonedes developed the aggregate-market paradigm, which implies that accounting produces numbers that have informational content dictated by market responses. To the counterarguments (1) that the procedures used to produce the numbers may induce market inefficiencies and (2) that recipients may be conditioned to respond to accounting numbers in a particular manner, Gonedes argued that if both cases were true, the opportunity for those who possess this knowledge to earn an abnormal profit would provide a basis for the demise of the market paradigm within the context of an efficient capital market.

In their award-winning paper, Gonedes and Dopuch provided a theoretical framework for assessing the desirability and effects of alternative accounting procedures. Their approach relies on the use of prices of (rates of returns on) firms' ownership shares. Gonedes and Dopuch concluded that the price-domain analysis is sufficient for assessing the effects of alternative accounting procedures or regulations but insufficient for assessing the desirability of alternative accounting procedures or regulations. This conclusion is based primarily on one case of market failure in which information of a public good nature cannot be excluded from nonpurchasers (the free-rider problem). In such a case, the prices of firms shares cannot be used to assess the desirability of alternative accounting procedures or regulations.

Among the market-failure possibilities is the issue of adverse selection.[44] Another is the effect of information on the completeness of markets and efficient risk-sharing arrangements.[45] Gonedes and Dopuch also noted that some criticisms of work based on capital-market efficiency, including the works of A. R. Abdel-Khalik and of Robert May and Gary Sundem, treat remarks on assessing effects as if they were remarks on assessing desirability.[46]

A contemporary piece of work by W. H. Beaver may also be viewed as an exemplar of the decision-usefulness/decision-maker/aggregate-market-behavior paradigm.[47] Beaver raised the issue of the importance of this relationship between accounting data and security behavior. He argued that it is inconceivable that optimal informational systems for investors can be selected without a knowledge of how accounting data are impounded in prices, because these prices determine wealth and wealth affects the multiperiod investment decisions of individuals.

Image of the Subject Matter

To those who adopt the decision-usefulness/decision-maker/aggregate-market-behavior paradigm, the basic subject matter is the aggregate-market response to accounting variables. These authors agree that in general the decision usefulness of accounting variables can be derived from aggregate-market-behavior, or as presented by Gonedes and Do-puch, only the effects of alternative accounting procedures or speculations can be assessed from aggregate-market behavior. According to Gonedes and Dopuch, the selection of the accounting-information system is determined by aggregate-market behavior.

Theories

The relationship between aggregate-market behavior and accounting variables is based on the theory of capital-market efficiency. According to this theory, the market for securities is deemed efficient in that (1) market prices "fully reflect" all publicly available information and, by implication, that (2) market prices are unbiased and respond instantaneously to new information. The theory implies that on the average, the abnormal return (the return in excess of the equilibrium expected return) to be earned from employing a set of extant information in conjunction with any trading scheme is zero.[48] This change in information set will automatically result in a new equilibrium. In fact the theories confirming the market behavior paradigm include: (1) the efficient market model,[49] (2) the efficient market hypothesis,[50] (3) the capital asset pricing model,[51] (4) the arbitrage pricing theory,[52] and (5) the equilibrium theory of option pricing.[53]

Methods

Those who accept the market paradigm rely on the following methods: (1) the market model,[54] (2) the beta estimation models,[55] (3) the event study methodology, (4) the Ohlson's Valuation model,[56] (5) the price-level balance sheet valuation models,[57] (6) the information content of earnings models,[58] and, (7) the models of the relation between earnings and return.[59]

THE DECISION-USEFULNESS/DECISION-MAKER/ INDIVIDUAL-USER PARADIGM

Exemplars

The work of William Bruns, may be considered the first exemplar of the decision-usefulness/decision-maker/individual-user paradigm.[60] Bruns proposed hypotheses that relate the use of accounting information, the relevance of accounting information to the decision maker's conception of accounting, and other available information to the effect of accounting information on decisions. These hypotheses are also developed in a model that identifies and relates some factors that may determine when decisions are affected by accounting systems and information. *Behavioral accounting research* is the study of how accounting functions and reports influence the behavior of accountants and nonaccountants.

Image of the Subject Matter

To those who adopt the decision-usefulness/decision-maker/individual-user paradigm, the basic subject matter is the individual-user response to accounting variables. Advocates of this paradigm argue that in general the decision usefulness of accounting variables may be derived from human behavior. In other words, accounting is viewed as a behavioral process. The objective of behavioral accounting research is to understand, explain, and predict human behavior within an accounting context. This paradigm is of interest to internal and external users of accounting, producers and attesters of information, and the general public or its surrogates.

Theories

Much of the research associated with the decision-usefulness/decision-maker/individual-user paradigm has been conducted without benefit of the explicit formation of a theory. In general, the alternative to developing appropriate behavioral accounting theories has been to borrow from other disciplines. Most of the honored theories adequately explain and predict human behavior within an accounting context. The resulting theories include: (1) cognitive relativism in accounting,[61] (2) cultural relativism in accounting,[62] (3) behavioral effects of accounting information,[63] (4) linguistic relativism in accounting,[64] (5) functional and data fixation hypotheses,[65] (6) information inductance hypotheses,[66] (7) organizational and budgeting slack hypotheses,[67] (8) contingency approaches to the design of accounting systems,[68] (9) participative budgeting and performance,[69] and (10) human information processing models.[70] They include the lens model,[71] the probalistic judgment model[72], the predecisional behavior model,[73] and the cognitive style approach.[74]

Models

Those accepting this paradigm tend to use all of the methods favored by behaviorists-observation techniques, interviews, and questionnaires, and experimentation is the preferred method. It is also a good starting point for further validation.

CONCLUSION

Accounting research is being conducted along various paradigms. They are basically: (1) the anthropological/inductive paradigm, (2) the true income/deductive paradigm, (3) the decision usefulness/decision model paradigm, (4) the market paradigm and (5) the behavioral paradigm. Each offers a unique vision of accounting theories, image of subject matter, methods, and results.

NOTES

1. Henry Rand Hatfield, "A Historical Defense of Bookkeeping," *The Journal of Accountancy* (April 1924), p. 241.

2. N. Eldredge and S. Gould, "Punctuated Equilibrium: An Alternative to Phyletic Gradualism," in T. J. Schoff, ed., *Models in Paleobiology* (San Francisco: Freeman, Cooper & Co., 1972), pp. 82–115.

3. Connie J. G. Gersick, "Revolutionary Change Theories: A Multilevel Exploration of the Punctuated Equilibrium Paradigm," *Academy of Management Review* 16 (1991), pp. 10–36.

4. T. S. Kuhn, *The Structure of Scientific Revolution* (Chicago: University of Chicago Press, 1962 [1st. ed], 1970 [2nd ed]).

5. Ibid., 2nd ed., p. 175.

6. Ibid., 1st ed., p. 6.

7. H. Gilman McCann, *Chemistry Transformed: The Paradigmatic Shift from Phlogiston to Oxygen* (Norwood, NJ: Ablex Publishing Corporation, 1978), p. 21.

8. Ibid., p. 13.

9. W. O. Hagstrom, *The Scientific Community* (New York: Basic Books, 1965), p. 17.

10. Ibid., p. 13.

11. R. K. Merton, "Priorities in Scientific Discovery: A Chapter in the Sociology of Science," *American Sociological Review* 22 (1957), p. 640.

12. R. K. Merton, "Behavior Patterns of Scientists," *American Scientist* 57 (1969), pp. 17–18.

13. Thomas S. Kuhn, "Reflections on My Critics," in Imre Lakatos and Alan Musgrave, eds., *Criticism and the Growth of Knowledge* (Cambridge: Cambridge University Press, 1970), pp. 231–78.

14. George Ritzer, "Sociology: A Multi-Paradigm Science," *American Sociologist* (August 1975), pp. 15–17.

15. Ibid., p. 15.

16. Ibid., p. 157.

17. Ross L. Watts and Jerold L. Zimmerman, *Positive Accounting Theory* (Englewood Cliffs, NJ: Prentice-Hall, 1986), p. 12.

18. American Accounting Association, Committee on Concepts and Standards for External Financial Reports, *Statement of Accounting Theory and Theory Acceptance* (Sarasota, FL: American Accounting Association, 1977).

19. R. R. Sterling, "On Theory Construction and Verification," *The Accounting Review* (July 1976), pp. 471–82.

20. S. Gilman, *Accounting Concepts of Profit* (New York: Ronald Press, 1927); Henry Rand Hatfield, *Accounting* (New York: D. Appleton, 1927); W. A. Paton and A. C. Littleton, *An Introduction to Corporate Accounting Standards*, Monograph No. 3 (Sarasota, FL: American Accounting Association, 1940); A. C. Littleton, *Structure of Accounting Theory*, Monograph No. 5 (Sarasota, FL: American Accounting Association, 1953); Y. Ijiri, *Theory of Accounting Measurement*, Studies in Accounting Research No. 10 (Sarasota, FL: American Accounting Association, 1975).

21. M. J. Gordon, "Postulates, Principles, and Research in Accounting," *The Accounting Review* (April 1964), pp. 251–63; R. L. Watts and J. L. Zimmerman, "Towards a Positive Theory of the Determination of Accounting Standards," *The Accounting Review* (January 1968), pp. 112–34.

22. Gordon, "Postulates, Principles and Research in Accounting," pp. 261–62.

23. Watts and Zimmerman, *Positive Accounting Theory*.

24. Gerald A. Felthman and Joel S. Demski, "The Use of Models in Information Evaluation," *The Accounting Review* (July 1969), pp. 457–66.

25. Stanley Baiman, "Agency Research in Managerial Accounting: A Survey," *Journal of Accounting Literature* (Spring 1982), p. 159.

26. C. R. Beidelman, "Income Smoothing: The Role of Management," *The Accounting Review* (October 1973), p. 653.

27. Watts and Zimmerman, *Positive Accounting Theory*.

28. A. Belkaoui and R. D. Picur, "The Smoothing of Income Numbers: Some Empirical Evidence on Systematic Differences between Core and Periphery Industrial Sectors," *The Journal of Business Finance and Accounting* (Winter 1984), pp. 527–46.

29. P. H. Dechow, R. G. Sloan, and A. P. Sweeney, "Detecting Earnings Management," *The Accounting Review* (April 1995), pp. 193–226.

30. Watts and Zimmerman, *Positive Accounting Theory*.

31. W. A. Paton, *Accounting Theory* (New York: Ronald Press, 1922); J. B. Canning, *The Economics of Accounting* (New York: Ronald Press, 1925); H. W. Sweeney, *Stabilized Accounting* (New York: Harper and Row, 1936); K. MacNeal, *Truth in Accounting* (Philadelphia: University of Pennsylvania Press, 1939); Sidney S. Alexander, "Income Measurement in a Dynamic Economy," *Five Monographs on Business Income* (New York: The Study Group on Business Income, The American Institute of Certified Public Accountants, 1950). See also E. O. Edwards and P. W. Bell, *The Theory and Measurement of Business Income* (Berkeley: University of California Press, 1961); Maurice Moonitz, "The Basic Postulates of Accounting," *Accounting Research Study No. 1* (New York: American Institute of Certified Public Accountants, 1961); R. T. Sprouse and M. Moonitz, "A Tentative Set of Broad Accounting Principles for Business Enterprises," *Accounting Research Study No. 3* (New York: American Institute of Certified Public Accountants, 1962).

32. McNeal, *Truth in Accounting*, p. 295.

33. Alexander, "Income Measurement in a Dynamic Economy," p. 159.

34. Perry Mason, *Price Level Changes and Financial Statements* (Sarasota, FL: American Accounting Association, 1971).

35. L. Revsine, *Replacement Cost Accounting* (Englewood Cliffs, NJ: Prentice-Hall, 1973).

36. G. Whittington, "Asset Valuation, Income Measurement and Accounting Income," *Accounting and Business Research* (Spring 1974), pp. 96–101.

37. R. J. Chambers, *Accounting, Evaluation, and Economic Behavior* (Englewood Cliffs, N.J: Prentice-Hall, 1966).

38. K. W. Lemke, "Asset Valuation and Income Theory," *The Accounting Review* (May 1966), pp. 33–41.

39. W. H. Beaver, J. W. Kennelly, and W. M. Voss, "Predictive Ability as a Criterion for the Evaluation of Accounting Data," *The Accounting Review* (October 1968), p. 675; R. R. Sterling, "Decision-Oriented Financial Accounting," *Accounting and Business Research* (Summer 1972), pp. 198–208.

40. Sterling, "Decision-Oriented Financial Accounting," p. 198.

41. Ibid., p. 109.

42. Ibid., p. 201.

43. N. J. Gonedes, "Efficient Capital Markets and External Accounting," *The Accounting Review* (January 1972), pp. 11–21; N. J. Gonedes and N. Do-

puch, "Capital-Market Equilibrium, Information Production and Selecting Accounting Techniques: Theoretical Frameworks and Review of Empirical Work," *Studies in Financial Accounting Objectives: 1974*, Supplement to *Journal of Accounting Research* 12 (1974), pp. 48–125.

44. M. Spence, "Job-Market Signaling," *Quarterly Journal of Economics* (August 1973), pp. 356–75.

45. Roy Rodner, "Competitive Equilibrium Under Uncertainty," *Econometrica* (January 1968), pp. 60–85.

46. A. R. Abdel-Khalik, "The Efficient Market Hypotheses and Accounting Data: A Point of View," *The Accounting Review* (October 1972), pp. 791–93; R. G. May and G. L. Sundem, "Cost of Information and Security Prices: Market Association Tests for Accounting Policy Decisions," *The Accounting Review* (January 1973), pp. 80–90.

47. W. H. Beaver, "The Behavior of Security Prices and Its Implications for Accounting Research (Methods)," in *Report of the Committee on Research Methodology in Accounting*, Supplement to *The Accounting Review* 47 (1972), pp. 407–37.

48. E. F. Fama, "The Behavior of Stock Market Prices," *Journal of Business* (January 1965), pp. 34–105.

49. W. H. Beaver, "Market Efficiency," *The Accounting Review* (January 1981), p. 28.

50. E. F. Fama, "Efficient Capital Markets: A Review of Theory and Empirical Work," *Journal of Finance* (May 1970), pp. 383–417.

51. W. F. Sharpe, "Capital-Asset Prices: A Theory of Market Equilibrium under Conditions of Risk," *Journal of Finance* (September 1974), pp. 425–42.

52. S. A. Ross, "The Arbitrage Theory of Capital Asset Pricing," *Journal of Economic Theory* (December 1976), pp. 341–60.

53. F. Black and M. Scholes, "The Pricing of Options and Corporate Liabilities," *Journal of Political Economy* (May/June 1973), pp. 637–54.

54. W. F. Sharpe, "A Simplified Model of Portfolio Approach," *Management Science* (January 1963), pp. 277–93.

55. S. N. Chen, and C. F. Lee, "Bayesian and Mixed Estimation of Time Varying Betas," *Journal of Economics and Business* (December 1982), pp. 291–301.

56. J. Ohlson, "Earnings, Book Values, and Dividends in Security Valuation," Working Paper, Columbia University, 1991.

57. M. Barth, "Relative Measurement Errors Among Alternative Pension Asset and Liability Measures," *The Accounting Review* (July 1991), pp. 433–63.

58. D. W. Collins and S. P. Kothari, "An Analysis of Intertemporal and Cross-Sectional Determinants of Earnings Response Coefficients," *Journal of Accounting and Economics* 11 (1989), pp. 143–81.

59. P. D. Easton and T. S. Harris, "Earnings as an Explanatory Variable for Returns," *Journal of Accounting Research* (Spring 1991), pp. 19–36.

60. William J. Bruns, Jr., "Accounting Information and Decision Making: Some Behavioral Hypotheses," *The Accounting Review* (July 1968), pp. 469–80.

61. Michael Gibbins, "Propositions about the Psychology of Professional Judgement in Public Accounting," *Journal of Accounting Research* (Spring 1984), pp. 103–25.

62. Ahmed Riahi-Belkaoui, *The Cultural Shaping of Accounting* (Westport, CT: Greenwood Press, 1995).

63. T. R. Dyckman, M. Gibbins, and R. J. Swieringa, "Experimental and Survey Research in Financial Accounting: A Review and Evaluation," in A. R. Abdel Khalik and T. F. Keller, eds., *The Impact of Accounting Research in Financial Accounting and Disclosure on Accounting Practice* (Durham, NC: Duke University Press, 1978), pp. 48–89.

64. Ahmed Riahi-Belkaoui, *The Linguistic Shaping of Accounting* (Westport, CT: Greenwood Press, 1996).

65. Ahmed Riahi-Belkaoui, "Accrual Accounting, Modified Cash Basis of Accounting and the Loan Decision: An Experiment in Functional Fixation," *Managerial Finance* 18, no. 5 (1992), pp. 3–13.

66. P. Prakash and A. Rappaport, "Information Inductance and Its Significance for Accounting," *Accounting, Organization and Society* (December 1982), p. 233.

67. Ahmed Riahi-Belkaoui, *Organizational and Budgetary Slack* (Westport, CT: Greenwood Press, 1994).

68. D. T. Otley, "The Contingency Theory of Management Accounting: Achievement and Prognosis," *Accounting, Organizations and Society* (December 1980), pp. 413–28.

69. Ahmed Riahi-Belkaoui, "The Effects of Goal Setting and Task Uncertainty on Task Outcomes," *Management Accounting Research* (June 1990), pp. 41–60.

70. Ahmed Riahi-Belkaoui, *Human Information Processing* (Westport, CT: Greenwood Press, 1989).

71. E. Brunswick, *The Conceptual Framework of Psychology* (Chicago: University of Chicago Press, 1952).

72. W. Edwards, "Conservatism in Human Information Processing," in B. Kleinmutz, ed., *Formal Representations of Human Judgement* (New York: Wiley, 1968).

73. J. N. Payne, M. L. Braunstein, and J. S. Caroll, "Exploring Predecisional Behavior: An Alternative Approach to Decision Research," *Organizational Behavior and Human Performance* (February 1978), pp. 17–44.

74. J. H. B. Huysman, "The Effectiveness of Cognitive Style Constraint in Implementing Operations Research Proposals," *Management Science* (September 1970), pp. 94–95.

SELECTED READINGS

Ball, Ray and George Foster. (1982). "Corporate Financial Reporting: A Methodological Review of Empirical Research." *Journal of Accounting Research*, Supplement 20, pp. 161–248.

Chow, Chee W. (Spring 1983). "Empirical Studies of the Economic Effects of Accounting Regulations on Security Prices: Finding, Problems, and Prospects." *Journal of Accounting Literature*, pp. 73–110.

Demski, Joel S. and David M. Kreps. (1982). "Models in Managerial Accounting." *Journal of Accounting Research*, Supplement 20, pp. 117–60.

Gersick, C.J.G. (1989). "Marking Time: Predictable Transitions in Task Groups." *Academy of Management Journal* 32, pp. 274–309.

Gersick, C.J.G. (1988). "Time and Transition in Work Teams: Towards a New Model of Group Development." *Academy of Management Journal* 31, pp. 9–41.

Gersick, C.J.G. and M. D. Davis. (1990). "Summary: Task Forces." In J. R. Hackman, ed., *Groups That Work (and those that don't): Creating Conditions for Effective Teamwork*. San Francisco: Jossey-Bass, pp. 146–53.

Gould, S. J. (1989). "Punctuated Equilibrium in Fact and Theory." *Journal of Social Biological Structure* 12, pp. 117–36.

Haken, H. (1981). "Synergetics: Is Self-organization Governed by Universal Principles?" In E. Jantsch, ed., *Toward a Unifying Paradigm of Physical, Biological, and Sociocultural Evolution*. Boulder, CO: Westview Press, pp. 15–23.

Kelly, Lauren (Spring 1983). "Positive Theory Research: A Review." *Journal of Accounting Literature*, pp. 111–50.

Kuhn, T. S. (1970). *The Structure of Scientific Revolution*, 2nd ed. Chicago: University of Chicago Press.

Lev, Baruch and James A. Ohlson. (1982). "Market-Based Empirical Research in Accounting: A Review, Interpretation, and Extension." *Journal of Accounting Research*, Supplement 20, pp. 161–234, 249–331.

Levinson, D. J. (1986). "A Conception of Adult Development." *American Psychologist* 41, pp. 3–13.

Levinson, D. J. (1978). *The Seasons of a Man's Life*. New York: Knopf.

McCann, H. Gilman. (1978). *Chemistry Transformed: The Paradigmatic Shift from Phlogiston to Oxygen*. Norwood, NJ: Alex Publishing Corporation.

Merton, R. K. (1957). "Priorities in Scientific Discovery: A Chapter in the Sociology of Science." *American Sociological Review* 22, pp. 635–59.

Swieringa, Robert J. and Karl E. Weick. (1982). "An Assessment of Laboratory Experiments in Accounting." *Journal of Accounting Research*, Supplement 20, pp. 56–116.

Watts, Ross L. and Jerold L. Zimmerman. (1986). *Positive Accounting Theory.* Englewood Cliffs, NJ: Prentice-Hall.

4
PERSPECTIVES ON STANDARD SETTING: THE ESSENCE OF A DECISION

The conduct of financial accounting rests on the accurate application of accounting standards. Therefore the enactment of accounting standards is an important decision as it affects the format and content of financial statements. The decision is essentially the domain of the Financial Accounting Standards Board (FASB). The way they make the decision is not observable. Yet there are documents, comment letters, and research papers that may give an indication of the factors that have affected the decision. The essence of the FASB decision in standard setting may in fact be viewed from different lenses. One model that has succeeded in formulating these lenses is G. T. Allison's model. It is used in this chapter to illustrate various visions in standard setting as a better way to comprehend the essence of the standard-setting decision.[1]

THE PRODUCTS AND OBJECTIVES OF STANDARD SETTING

The Products of Standard Setting

Standard setting is merely the enactment of standards by the accounting standard-setting body of a given country. The content of the standard may vary from one standard to another. There are, however, three aspects of a standard that seemed to be prevalent: (1) a description of the nature of accounting problem; (2) an elaboration on the various ways of addressing and correcting the problem, sometimes using some form of fundamental theory; and (3) a statement of the solution chosen and the rationale for such choice.[2] When the standards are restricted to point 3, they are generally ad hoc standards devoid of any theoretical rationale to be used for their support. When standards include the theory part, they have a better chance to be legitimized and used in practice.

In considering the subject matter of standards, H. C. Edey divides requirements under standards into four main types.[3]

1. *Type 1* states that accountants must tell people what they are doing by disclosing the methods and assumptions (accounting policies) they have adopted.

2. *Type 2* aims at achieving some uniformity of presentation of accounting statements.

3. *Type 3* calls for the disclosure of specific matters in which the user may be called to exercise his or her own judgement.

4. *Type 4* requires implicit or explicit decisions to be made about approved asset valuation and income determination.

Are standards of type 4—first, based on broad, debated principles and on a comparison of the pros and cons of rival theories and, second, selected on that basis by an authority (a standard setting body)—possible? Many people will express serious doubt. In any case, all these types of standards continue to be promulgated. Some good reasons to establish standards are that they:

1. Provide users of accounting information with information about the financial position, performance, and conduct of a firm. This information is assumed to be clear, consistent, reliable, and comparable.

2. Provide public accountants with guidelines and rules of action to enable them to exercise due care and independence in selling their expertise and integrity in auditing firms' reports and in attesting the validity of these reports.

3. Provide the government with databases on variables that are deemed essential to the conduct of taxation, regulation of enterprises, planning and regulation of the economy, and enhancement of economic efficiency and other social goals.[4]

4. Generate interest in principles and theories among all those interested in the accounting disciplines. The mere promulgation of a standard generates a lot of controversy and debate both in practice and in academic circles, which is better than apathy.[5]

The Objectives of Standard Setting

The standard setters making a decision on a standard are in fact making a social choice decision requiring political bargaining and the search for an agreement. To insure its legitimacy the nonelected standard-setting body needs to rely on the right objectives in the process of standard setting. Two approaches exist: (1) a representational faithfulness approach, and (2) an economic consequences approach.

The first approach tries to eliminate all biases and favors the search for neutral reporting and faithful representations through the standard-setting process. It can be easily compared to a financial map-making that requires that maps be accurate and faithful. The second approach aims to enact standards that have economic consequences in the sense that they have a positive, or at least nonnegative, impact on social welfare.[6] A new approach that is finding more and more supporters argues for the recognition of an explicit political economy of accounting that views both the positive and negative social implications of standard setting.[7,8,9]

The Procedures of Standard Setting

Since its inception, the FASB has adopted the following due-process procedures:

1. A reporting problem is identified and placed on the Board's agenda.
2. A task force composed of a group of knowledgeable individuals in the accounting and business community is appointed. The technical staff of the FASB, in consultation with the task force, prepares a Discussion Memorandum (DM) on the reporting problem. The DM exposes the principal questions and alternatives to be considered by the board.
3. The DM is made available to the public for examination for a period of at least 60 days.
4. A public hearing is staged, during which viewpoints regarding the merits and limitations of various possible positions are presented to the Board.
5. Based on the oral and written comments received, the Board issues an Exposure Draft (ED) of a Proposed Statement of Financial Accounting Standards. Unlike the DM, the ED sets forth the definite position of the Board on the reporting problem.
6. The ED is made available to the public for examination for a period of at least 30 days.

7. Another public hearing is staged, during which viewpoints regarding the merits and limitations of the positions set forth in the ED are presented to the Board.

8. Based again on the oral and written comments received following the issuance of the ED, the board may take any of the following actions:

   a. Adopt the Proposed Standard as an Official Statement of Financial Accounting Standards (SFAS).

   b. Propose a revision of the proposed standard, again following the due-process procedure.

   c. Postpone the issuance of a standard and keep the problem on the agenda.

   d. Not issue a standard, and eliminate the issue from the agenda.

Public participation does not alter the fact that the actual decisions regarding accounting standards are made by the members of the FASB.

Legitimacy of the Standard-Setting Process

Producing an optimal accounting system is one of the most important conditions for the legitimacy of the standard-setting process. The optimal accounting system would be "one for which the expected payoff to a user employing an optimal decision strategy is greater than or equal to the corresponding payoff for any other alternative system."[10] What it implies is that a better user utility is not possible with any alternative system. Can such an optimal system be attained? A pessimistic view was created by Joel Demski's use of the impossibility theorem to argue that (1) an accounting standard-setting process must satisfy K. Arrow's condition[11] to be legitimate; and (2) no set of standards exists that will always seek alternatives in accordance with preferences and beliefs.[12] Demski concludes as follows: "We have interpreted accounting theory as providing a complete and transitive ranking of accounting alternatives at the individual level. It was then proven that no set of standards (applied to the accounting alternative per se) exist that will rank accounting alternatives in relation to consistent individual preferences and beliefs."[13]

This pessimistic prognosis was expanded to show (1) that the selection of financial reporting alternatives ultimately must entail trading off one person's gain for another,[14] and (2) that the resolution of financial reporting alternatives will require "value or ethical judgements as to whose well-being will be traded off—and in what dimensions for whose."[15]

What appears from these efforts is that rational choice theory offers no hope for solutions to the issues of choice among financial reporting alternatives.[16]

In fact, Barry Cushing gave an optimistic prognosis about the sheer responsibility of optimal accounting principles, provided that the assumption of heterogeneous users is dropped, and that the assumptions underlying the Arrow Paradox are challenged, namely the assumptions (1) that Arrow's definition of a social welfare function requires that social choices be transitive, and (2) that Arrow's condition of "independence or irrelevant alternatives" is of questionable merit.[17]

Another optimistic prognosis is offered by Michael Bromwich on the possibility of partial accounting standards—standards for one or more accounting problems, enacted in isolation from standards or other accounting problems.[18] R. J. Chambers chose to counteract Demski's economic school and impossibility thesis by proposing a necessity school that assumes the existence of an ideal norm or standard that cuts across specific situations.[19] The norm is the information that represents the current money and money's worth of assets and the amount currently owning to others at any time.[20] Even if that norm is not available, Chambers suggests that the feasible alternative that most closely produces the necessary measure is the preferred alternative.

Cushing, Chambers, and Bromwich, in demonstrating that under certain restrictive conditions it was possible to select accounting standards without isolating Arrow's conditions (or by violating only some minor aspects of one or more conditions), could have argued the legitimacy of the FASB by focusing on its feasibility and the irrelevancy of Arrow's Impossibility Theorem of the assessment of the legitimacy of the FASB standard-setting process. They would have used G. Tullock's argument when he examines the relevance of Arrow's Impossibility Theorem for purposes of assessing the legitimacy of certain voting processes, and concluded in these terms:

One of the real problems raised by Arrow's look was why the real world democracies seemed to function fairly well in spite of the logical impossibility of rationally aggregating preferences. (Although) no decision process will meet Arrow's criteria perfectly, many (processes) meet them for a very high degree of approximation (and, therefore, the ability of a process to meet the strictly mathematical requirements imposed by Arrow is largely irrelevant in the real world).[21]

The problem remaining, however, is to assert the legitimacy of the FASB. To achieve that task, S. B. Johnson and D. Solomons relied on the "individualistic constitutional calculus."[22] This process involved mainly the economics/political science literature.[23] It is defined as follows:

Individualistic constitutional calculus is based on the premise that a process or institution is legitimate if it continues to be acceptable to its constituency in spite of the Challenges posed to its credibility by the inevitable crisis that surrounds the exercise of such authority. In short, legitimacy implies acceptability in the face of uncertainty, and that, in turn, implies institutional durability.[24]

Basically, institutional constitutional calculus established the legitimacy of the FASB based on (1) its ability to provide adequate procedural safeguard; (2) its ability to impose constraints on the choice set that are adequate to ensure an acceptable outcome; and (3) the balance of procedural and outcome controls possessed by the standard-setting process of the FASB. The ability of the FASB to meet these conditions was assessed by showing that the FASB possess sufficient authority, ensure substantive due process, and ensure procedural due process.[25]

RESPONSIBILITY FOR STANDARD SETTING

Theories of Regulation

Each industry requires some form of regulation for its own benefit. Examples of theories of regulation include: (1) public interest theories, and (2) interest group or capture theories.[26,27] In the case of public interest theories of regulation, the need for a supply of regulation is triggered by the demand of the public for the correction of inefficient and inequitable market prices. The specific regulation is intended for the protection and benefit of the general public. In the case of interest group or capture theories, the need for a supply of regulation is triggered by the demand of special interest groups with the objective function of maximizing their members' income. The main reasons of the theory are: (1) the political ruling-elite theory of regulation,[28] and (2) the economic theory of regulation.[29] The political ruling-elite theory concerns the use of political power to gain regulatory control; the economic theory concerns economic power.

Which of these theories better describes accounting standard setting?

Unfortunately, the theory of what constitutes maximizing behavior in an accounting regulatory agency is in its infancy. George Benston attempted to explain the behavior of the Securities and Exchange Commission (SEC) according to the economic theory's predictions of agency conservatism.[30] Needless to say, this view by Benston has been inconsistent with the behavior of the SEC since the early 1970s. Similarly, M. E. Hussein and J. E. Ketz examined and rejected the plausibility of the political ruling-elite version of the theory of regulation.[31] More empirical evidence is needed to develop a theory of regulation of accounting standards.

Is Standard Setting Needed?

A debate exists as to whether accounting should or should not be regulated. Those arguing for an unregulated market use agency theory to question why incentives should exist for reliable and voluntary reporting to owners. To solve the conflict between owners and managers, financial reporting is used to monitor employment contracts, to judge and reward managers. In addition, firms have an incentive to report voluntarily to the capital market, because they compete for resources with other firms in a competitive capital market, and failure to report might be interpreted as bad news. Even if firms do not report voluntarily, those seeking the information may resort to private contractors for the information.

Those arguing for a regulated market use a public interest argument. Basically, either market failures or the need to achieve social goals dictate a regulation of accounting. Market failures, as suboptimal allocation of issuances, may be the result of (1) a firm's reluctance to disclose information about itself, as it is a monopoly supplier of information about itself; (2) the occurrence of fraud; or (3) the underproduction of accounting information as a public good. The need to achieve desired social goals also argues for a regulation of accounting. These goals include fairness of reporting, information symmetry, and the protection of investors, to name only a few.

The Free-Market Approach

The free-market approach to the production of standards starts from the basic assumption that accounting information is an economic good, much the same as other goods or services. As such it is subject to the forces of demand by interested users, and supply by interested preparers. What results is an optimal amount of information disclosed at an optimal price.

Whenever a given piece of information is needed and the right price is offered for it, the market will generate the information if the price exceeds the cost of the information. The market is thus presented as the ideal mechanism for determining the types of information to be disclosed, the recipients of the information, and the accounting standards to govern the production of such information.

Advocates of a regulatory approach (whether private or public) maintain that there are both *explicit* and *implicit* market failures in the private market for the information. In general, *explicit market failure* is assumed to happen when either the quantity or the quality of a good produced in an unregulated market differs from the private costs of and benefits derived from that good, and the market solution results in a non-Pareto resource allocation. The same explicit market failure is also applied to the private market for the accounting information, with the assumption that the quality and quantity of the accounting information differ from the social optimum. More explicitly, accounting information is viewed as a public good, and due to the inability to exclude nonpurchasers (free riders) there is a non-Pareto optimal production of the information of firms.[32]

Implicit market failure theories focus on one or more of the following claimed defects of the private markets for accounting information: monopoly control over information by management, naive investors, functional fixation, misleading numbers, diversity of procedures, and lack of objectivity.[33] Each of these alleged defects is briefly examined next.

Monopoly control over information by management: the hypothesis claims that accountants possess a monopolistic influence over the data provided and used by the market. As a result, the market cannot really distinguish between real and accounting effects, and may be misled by the accounting changes.[34]

Naive investors: the hypothesis claims that those investors who are not well versed in some of the complex accounting techniques and transformations may be "fooled" by the use of different techniques by comparable firms and may not be able to adjust their decision-making process to take the diversity of accounting procedures into account.

Functional fixation: it is argued that under certain conditions investors may be unable to change their decision-making processes in response to a change in the underlying accounting process that provided them with the data. The failure of these investors to change their decision-making processes to conform to a change in accounting methods is attributed to the phenomenon of functional fixation.

Misleading numbers: because accounting relies heavily on various asset valuation bases and various allocation procedures deemed arbitrary and incorrigible, the accounting output is at best meaningless or misleading, for the purpose of decision-making.

Diversity of procedures: given the flexibility in the choice of accounting techniques used to report particular events and the inclination of management to present a "desired" picture, the accounting output from one firm to another firm is less than comparable and useful.

Lack of objectivity: no objectivity criteria are available on which management can base its choice of accounting techniques: incomparable output is the obvious result.

Based on these alleged defects, those who favor some form of regulation of accounting criticize the market approach as ineffective and claim that regulation is superior in improving accounting output. These allegations have not gone uncontested. The best challenge to the market failure theories as they affect accounting information is summarized by R. W. Leftwich:

Market failure theories contain a fundamental flaw. The output identified by those theories as optimal is optimal in name only—it is defined independently of any institutional arrangements, that can produce the output. None of these theories identifies a level of output which is optimal, given the existing technology of markets, regulations or any other regimes. Thus, unless market failure theories incorporate attainable institutional arrangements, they can yield no policy implication. It is illogical to condemn the actual output of an existing market (or government agency) merely because the quantity or quality of that output differs from an unattainable norm that is falsely described as optimal.[35]

The question of what would happen to financial accounting in the absence of regulation remains. Homer Kripke proposes the following two possible consequences:

First, there would continue to be adequate accounting disclosures, as issuers negotiated with lenders, investors, and underwriters in the new issue market and felt the pressure of analysts, in the trading market. Second, the accounting would be less uniform than it is now, because vast differences in views as to the appropriate interpretation and abstraction of events are concealed by the mandated system. But the pressure would be such that the disclosure would be adequate to enable the reader to make his own judgement.[36]

The Private-Sector Approach

The private-sector approach to the regulation of accounting standards rests on the fundamental assumption that the public interest in accounting is best served if standard setting is left to the private sector. Private standard setting in the United States has included the Committee on Accounting Procedures (1939–59), and the Financial Accounting Standards Board (1973–present). Given that the FASB is the ongoing, standard-setting body in the private sector, it will be used to illustrate the advantages and the limitations of private-sector regulation of accounting standards.

Advocates of the private-sector approach cite the following arguments in support of their position:

1. The FASB seems to be responsive to various constituents. First, it is composed of members of various interested groups in addition to the public accounting profession. Second, its financial support is derived from the contributions of diverse groups of individuals, companies, and associations. Third, it has adopted a complex due-process procedure that relies heavily on the responses of all interested constituents. Fourth, the due-process procedure generates an active concern about the consequences of its actions on the constituents

2. The FASB seems to be able to attract, as members or as staff, people who possess the necessary technical knowledge to develop and implement alternative measurement and disclosure systems. As a unit, the standards are more likely to be acceptable to certified public accountant (CPA) firms, business firms, and external users.

3. The FASB seems to be successful in generating responses from its constituency base and in responding to such input. The volume of responses to controversial topics shows that the constituents have been expressing interest by participating and voicing their concern through at least three different mediums: (1) written responses to a discussion memorandum, (2) oral responses to an exposure draft, and (3) written responses to an exposure draft. Such participation is deemed essential to the accounting standard-setting process. A former staff member of the FASB describes the importance of the constituents' input:

The FASB represents a legislative body in the private sector that must pay careful attention to the views of all the elements of its constituency. Each constituent potentially affects formulation of the FASB decisions by providing thoughtful and theoretically sound input for the board members to comprehend and evaluate, weigh against other constituent input, and synthesize with their own educated views on the particular issue of concern. The decision-making process, however, does not merely involve tallying these constituent preferences and resolving the issue by majority consensus. The FASB's responsibility in reaching its decision entails careful consideration of all constituent interest; it does not entail numerical-count comparisons or attempts to serve specific constituents over others.[37]

Opponents of the private-sector approach cite the following arguments in support of their position:

1. The FASB lacks statutory authority and enforcement power and faces the challenge of an override by either Congress or a governmental agency. Robert Kaplan states the case as follows: "Acceptance of FASB standards requires voluntary agreement from the AICPA [American Institute of CPAs] and the benevolent delegation of authority from the SEC. Lacking true statutory authority, the private standard setting agency is always susceptible to end runs by aggrieved constituents when they feel their particular ox is about to be gored."[38] This situation is a result of the positions taken by Congress and the SEC on accounting standard-setting. Following the Securities Acts of 1933 and 1934, Congress became the legal authority for standard setting. It then delegated its authority to the accounting profession. Finally, in Accounting Series Release No. 150, the SEC recognized the authoritative nature of the pronouncements of the FASB and at the same time retained its role as adviser and supervisor as a constant threat of override.

2. The FASB is often accused of lacking independence from its large constituents: public accounting firms and corporations. This lack of independence translates into a lack of responsiveness to the public interest. This theme gained popularity as a result of assertions made in the Metcalf Report that the accounting and financial reporting standard-setting process is dominated by the "big eight" accounting firms.[39] One way in which this domination may manifest itself is through pressure in the FASB to avoid standards that would involve subjective estimates, especially standards that would require the use of current-market prices. Kaplan states the case as follows:

Because practitioners from CPA firms are primarily auditors, the auditing implications of any standard will receive a great deal of attention from a private standard setting agency. There will be strong pressure for rules that can be implemented without requiring subjective estimates that are difficult to audit and even more difficult to defend should the financial statements be subject to question in a judicial proceeding. Given the present litigious climate, auditors wish to avoid having to certify figures for which objective verifiable evidence is unavailable. These feelings are reinforced by corporate executives, another principal constituency of the private standard setting agency, who may also fear the repercussions from issuing "soft" data. In addition, the production of subjective data is expensive and introduces a degree of uncontrolled volatility to a company's financial statements.[40]

3. The FASB is often accused of responding slowly to major issues that are of crucial importance to some of its constituents. This situation is generally attributed to the length of time required for due process and extensive deliberations of the Board. The defenders of the Board maintain, however, that these extensive deliberations may allow the Board to correct the unintended side effects of some of its pronouncements. This brings to mind the additional problem that the proposed standards have a slim chance of being implemented without general support. Charles Horngren provides the following details on problems associated with the Accounting Principles Board's (APB) issuance in October 1971 of an exposure draft supporting the deferral method:

Without public support, which usually means without the widespread support of industry, significant changes are seldom possible. Perhaps the situations would be better expressed negatively. If there is widespread hostility to a suggested accounting principal, there is a small chance of implementing it—regardless of how impeccable or how heavy the support within the board.

The investment tax credit is a clear example of the impotency of both the SEC and the APB when hostility is rampant. Let me describe the events without getting tangled in the pros and cons of the conceptual issues:

The APB did not use its exposure draft of October 22, 1971, until receiving two written commitments. The SEC said it would support the APB position, and the Department of the Treasury indicated that it "will remain neutral in the matter." The Senate Finance Committee issued its version of the 1971 Revenue Act of November 9. In response to lobbying, the committee clearly indicated that companies should have a free choice in selecting the accounting treatment of the new credit.

On November 12, the Treasury sent a letter to the chairman of the Senate Finance Committee that stated: "Since any change in the preexisting, well-established financial accounting practice might operate to diminish the job-creating effect of the credit, the Treasury Department strongly supports a continuation of the optimal treatment." Congress then cut the ground out from under the APB and the SEC by passing legislation that stated: "No taxpayer shall be required, without his consent, to use . . . any particular method of accounting for the credit."

The APB's unanimous denunciation of congressional involvement was issued on December 9, 1971.[41]

The Public-Sector Approach

Public-sector regulation of any activity is always the subject of heated debate between advocates and opponents. Without a doubt, public-sector regulation has gained a high degree of legitimacy and has become part of American and international traditions and legal frameworks. To be effective, however, regulation must ascribe to certain general principles. R. K. Elliot and W. Schuetze present the following:

First, regulation must not violate constitutional rights or statutes. Second, it should be designed to prevent real or probable social change. Third, regulation must be in the public interest. A corollary to this principle is that costs must not exceed benefits and the regulation itself ought not to be superfluous. If the forces of the market place can resolve a question adequately, regulation is superfluous. Fourth, regulation should not be adopted by the public sector if its purpose can be achieved by private-sector institutions. Fifth, the potential regulatee should not bear the burden of proving regulation is warranted; rather, advocates of regulation must demonstrate that regulation is warranted. Sixth, regulatory action should not be used to correct occasional lawbreaking, which is the task of law enforcement; nor should regulatory responsibilities be established to combat occasional antisocial behavior that can be proscribed by statute.[42]

Even if all of these principles were met, regulation is still perceived to be suffering from various failures. J. W. Buckley and P. O'Sullivan identify the following four as some of the observed regulatory failures: the zero-cost phenomenon, which results from the fact that regulators do not bear the costs of their failures; the regulatory lag or nonfeasance, which results from delays in regulation; the regulatory trap, which refers to the difficulties of reversing a given regulation; and the tar-baby effect, which results from the tendency of regulation to expand continually.[43]

Given these strong arguments about regulation in general, what about public-sector regulation of accounting specifically? As we might expect, arguments for and against public-sector regulation of accounting standards abound in the literature. These arguments center generally around the role of the SEC.

Advocates of public-sector regulation of accounting standards cite the following arguments in favor of their position:

1. It is generally maintained that the process of innovation in accounting rests on the role of a governmental agency such as the SEC as a "creative irritant."[44] The implication here is that the SEC is the most important catalyst for change, and that the private sector and market forces do not provide the leadership necessary to effect such change. The SEC has been instrumental in guiding the field from "safe" or "conservative" methods of accounting toward more innovative and realistic methods of accounting.

2. It is argued that the structure of securities regulation established by the Securities Acts of 1933 and 1934 serves to protect investors against perceived abuses. Thus public-sector regulation of accounting standards is motivated by the need to protect the public interest. It provides mechanisms to offset the preparer bias that institutionally exists in the standard-setting process, as well as to offset the economic limitations of investors seeking adequate information.[45] The mechanisms include suggestions through speeches, the exercise of rule-making powers granted by Congress under the Securities Acts of 1933 and 1934, the use of a review and comment process, and the power not to accelerate the effectiveness of a registration statement and to discourage accounting applications in cases judged to be inappropriate, given the circumstances.[46]

3. The SEC is motivated by the desire to create a level of public disclosure deemed necessary and adequate for decision making.[47] To do so the SEC assumes the role of advocate for investors and attempts to determine their needs by continuously surveying analysts and other interested users.

4. Unlike the FASB, the SEC has secured greater legitimacy through its explicit statutory authority. Added to that is a greater enforcement power than a private agency and the absence of an explicit constituency that may be concerned.[48] In short, the SEC is better able to conduct experiments in disclosure policy when they are enforceable and can go uncontested by all participants in the standard-setting process.

5. Some claim that the private sector has to be watched and controlled, given that its objectives may sometimes contradict the public interest. A minimum of governmental intervention is deemed necessary to avoid the extreme and negative behaviors.[49]

There are, however, strong arguments against public-sector regulation of accounting standards:

1. It is generally maintained that there is a high corporate cost for compliance with government regulation of information. The problem is a matter of concern to opponents of public-sector regulation of accounting standards. The financial reports required by the federal government keep increasing to comply with such legislation as the Sherman Act, the Robinson-Patman Act, Department of Energy pricing rules, and all of the other government agencies that require detailed financial reports. All of these reports have an impact on business organization in terms of paper costs and constant changes in organizational structure that cause the formation of new position or departments. Added to these complaints are the following as yet unanswered questions: What happens to the reports once they are sent to the federal government? Do they end up in some agency's files never to be looked at again? Or is the information from this one company's reports actually used, along with that from thousands of other corporations, to make important policy decisions? A study of attempting to follow up on some of this information and see what happens to it would be interesting. Perhaps such a study would also give some indication of the possible benefits to society from such information-gathering.[50]

2. Some have argued that bureaucrats have a tendency to maximize the total budget of their bureau.[51] Applied to the SEC, this argument assumes that the SEC is staffed with people who tend to maximize their own welfare with no consideration for the costs and benefits of additional disclosures.[52]

3. There is the danger that standard-setting may become increasingly politicized. Special interest groups may possess the added initiative to lobby the governmental agency for special treatment. Moreover, political appointees may feel that "witch hunts" are necessary to protect the public interest. Another fear is that "uninformed populists" may want some of the action at the expense of accounting standards and the accounting profession.[53]

4. Some have questioned the need for a governance system backed by police power. It is claimed that such a situation may hinder the conduct of research and experimentation of accounting policy and is not essential to achieve standardization of measurement.[54]

STANDARD SETTING USING ALLISON'S APPROACH

Two techniques, full costing and successful efforts costing, have long been used by oil and gas companies to account for costs incurred in the exploration, development, and production of crude oil and natural gas.[55]

The main difference between the two techniques relates to the accounting for those costs that cannot be directly related to the discovery of specific oil and gas reserves. Under full costing they are capitalized, while under successful-efforts costing they are expensed. The choice of a standard acceptable to all interested parties has been a controversial issue for many years in the United States.

Following the strong and widespread reaction triggered by its oil and gas July 1977 exposure draft, the FASB issued on December 5, 1977, the Statement of Financial Accounting Standards no. 19 which specified that oil- and gas-producing activities must be accounted for under the "successful-efforts" costing method. The opposition by various parties to the requirements of SFAS No. 19 prompted the Securities and Exchange Commission, through its Accounting Series Releases (ASR) No. 253, to nullify SFAS No. 19. Why did the FASB adopt the "successful-efforts" costing method? This section analyzes the FASB's decision to adopt the successful-efforts costing method in SFAS No. 19. The framework of analysis used is the series of conceptual models developed by Allison (1971) in his *Essence of a Decision*, namely Model I, Model II, and Model III.[56] In what follows, each of the models is used to explain the decision of the FASB to adopt the successful-efforts costing method in SFAS No. 19. A critical evaluation of the Allison approach is then presented.

The Rational Actor Approach

Allison's Model I is the *rational actor* model. It takes as its basic unit of analysis the organization's action as rational choice. The action or choice it takes amounts to a maximization of the goals, values, and objectives. It is a rational choice in the sense that it "consists of value-maximizing adaptation within the context of a *given* payoff function, *fixed* alternatives, and consequences that are *known*."[57]

The rational choice can be an optimal choice given an assumption of comprehensive rationality when the decision maker knows totally the payoff function by an accurate mapping of all the consequences in terms of the agent's value, all the alternatives, and all the consequences.[58] A sure acceptable assumption would be of course the one of limited rationality restricting clauses of optimal choice. To use the "rational actor" model to explain an organization's action, the analyst identifies the correct goals, alternatives, and consequences by putting himself or herself in the place of the organization. This procedure is applied here to the FASB's choice in SFAS No. 19.

The Energy Policy and Conservation Act charged the SEC with implementing oil and gas accounting standards; by December 22, 1977, this task was delegated to the FASB. The FASB was faced with at least two fixed alternatives, full-costing method and successful-efforts method, and some consequences that are known. The situation appearing to the FASB members was expressed in *Accounting Research Study no. 11*,[59] industry's position as expressed by John Myers' study,[60] and the Federal Power Commission's position as expressed by order no. 440.[61] At the same time the FASB was involved in its efforts to develop a Conceptual Framework for Accounting and in establishing the objectives of general-purpose external financial reporting by business enterprises. Both projects were intended as an expression of the goals and objectives of financial accounting. The first objective states:

Financial reporting should provide information that is useful to present and potential investors and creditors and other users in making rational investment, credit, and similar decisions. The information should be comprehensible to those who have a reasonable understanding of business and economic activities and are willing to study the information with reasonable diligence.[62]

What is considered of value by the FASB is the presentation of financial statements as an important source of information about companies' risk and returns. These goals of the FASB to develop a conceptual framework and establish the objectives of financial accounting may be interpreted as a desire to protect the public interest in general and the average user in particular by providing them with relevant information for assessing the companies' risk and returns.

Given these goals or objectives of the FASB, the oil and gas accounting treatment most likely to achieve them appears to be the successful-efforts method. Consider the following arguments:

1. Financial statements should reflect risk and unsuccessful results.[63] Because it capitalized the cost of unsuccessful efforts, the full-costing method does not highlight these characteristics. "Successful-efforts accounting, on the other hand, highlights failures and the risks involved in the search for oil and gas reserves by charging to expense costs that are known not to have resulted in identifiable future benefits."[64]

2. The ability to raise capital is not reduced by adopting the successful-efforts method. First, in a free market system capital is attracted by

successful firms if the investors are capable of determining whether the expected returns are commensurate with the risks involved. Second, a 1972 survey showed that firms using the successful-efforts method accounted for nearly 85% of U.S. oil and gas production and full-costing as favored mostly by small and medium-sized firms.[65] Third, a 1973 survey of approximately 300 oil and gas firms showed that roughly half used the successful-efforts method.[66] Fourth, of 79 oil and gas companies with securities traded on an exchange, 41% were identified by the staff of the FASB as using successful-efforts accounting. Fifth, in the telephone interview survey conducted by Professor Horace R. Block, none of the 27 executive officers of publicly owned successful-efforts companies felt that this accounting method had hindered its ability to raise capital.[67] Similarly, the majority of 24 bank loan officers, bank trust department officers, and securities underwriters indicated that "the method of accounting would not affect their investment and credit decisions regarding oil and gas producing companies."[68] Sixth, the market researches conducted by Thomas Dyckman[69] in cooperation with Abbie Smith and the FASB staff and by the Directorate of Economic and Policy Research of the SEC appeared to support the contention that the proposed elimination of full-cost accounting had no apparent permanent adverse effects on the security returns of full-cost firms. D. W. Collins and W. T. Dent raised a number of questions regarding sample selection and the propriety of statistical procedures used in these analyses.[70]

3. The "cover" concept is inconsistent with the accounting framework. Under the full costing method, the value of the previously discovered reserves may be used to "cover" for unsuccessful acquisition and exploration costs and hence no loss is to be recognized. Such a treatment obscures the real risk to investors.

These arguments and possibly others provide strong and favorable, conceptual and empirical arguments for the desirability of the successful-efforts costing method. Because the FASB's objectives are to be consistent with the accounting framework, and present adequate information on which investment, lending, and other related decisions may be made, *the successful-efforts costing method appears as a consistent value-maximizing choice.*

The Organizational Process Approach

Allison's Model II is the *organizational process* model. What Model I views as "acts" or "choices" are viewed by Model II as "output" of organizations regulated by standard patterns of behavior. The emphasis is the organization's action as organizational output. The action or choice it takes results from some established standard rules, procedures, and repertoires of the organization. As well explained by J. D. Cheshire and E. H. Feroz:

The core of this model is the output based on standard operating procedures (SOP). Behavior is predetermined by SOP. Goals are not achieved by maximizing values but by operating within a preestablished set of performance criteria. The process of coordinating past, present and future events to a consistent decision base is an important factor in the model. Another element of the model is that uncertainty is dealt with by conformity. If one is uncertain as to the reliability and consequences of a decision then he/she will conform to the confines of a predetermined organizational standard. The emphasis on conformity in this model does not mean that the decisions will not have a sound base. It means that the perspective from which the rationale is drawn is derived from preestablished guidelines as opposed to considering decisions independently and in their own right as in the rational actor model.[71]

Applied to this study, an examination of the accounting issues and the derived accounting standards as "output" of the FASB may show the establishment of standard operating procedures and repertoires and may therefore explain the position taken in SFAS No. 19 to adopt the successful-efforts costing method. The issues to be examined will include research and development, leases and contingencies, and will be limited to the asset and liability recognition.

In SFAS No. 2 the Board decision was that research and development expenditures should be expensed in all cases.[72] Research and development seemed to fit the definition of an asset given by the Board as "a scarce resource for which there is expectation of future benefits to the enterprise."[73] However, the Board argued that research and development benefits may be considered highly uncertain as to existence, amount, and timing, which justifies a different accounting treatment than conventional assets. The Board mentions as a supporting argument the result of one study of a number of industries which found that an average of less than 255 of new product ideas and less than 15% of product development projects were commercially successful.[74]

In SFAS No. 5 the Board decision was that a loss contingency should be recognized if and only if both of the following conditions are met: (1) information available prior to the issuance of financial statements indicates that it is probable that an asset has been impaired or that a liability has been incurred, and (2) the amount of loss can be reasonably estimated. Thus, if a loss contingency is probable and can be reasonably estimated, it should be accrued.

In SFAS No. 13 the Board decision was that a lease which "transfers substantially all of the benefits and risks incidental to the ownership of property should be accounted for as the acquisition of an asset and as a sale or financing by a lessor."[75] Thus a lease which transfers substantially all of the benefits and risks of ownership constitutes an event with highly uncertain and measurable consequences to be accounted for as an asset.

In conclusion, the three standards expressed by SFAS Nos. 2, 5, and 13 reflect a definition of an asset (liability) as an expression of minimum benefits (commitments). Teddy Coe and George Sorter reach a similar conclusion as evidenced by the following statement: "We must conclude that the Board seems to believe that a necessary condition for the existence of an asset is 'the virtual assurance of minimal benefits' at the time of expenditures."[76] Accordingly, the successful-efforts costing method appears as an "output" of the FASB regulated by standard operating procedures and repertoires, namely in terms of only recognizing an asset when there is a "virtual assurance of minimal benefits" at the time of expenditures.

The Political Approach

In a Model III analysis, the identification of the perceptions, power, positions, and maneuvers of each of the major players is used to explain the chosen alternatives with each player acting on their own perception of the issue through a psychopolitical bargaining power. The adoption of the successful-efforts costing method in SFAS No. 19 may be viewed as a political *resultant* in a struggle involving the members of the FASB, the SEC, the accounting profession, the oil and gas companies, and other regulatory agencies.

SFAS No. 19 was adopted by the affirmative votes of only four members of the Board. The three members who dissented argued that (1) it is necessary to account for mineral reserves at fair value for the financial statements to appropriately emphasize certain economic characteristics of the industry; (2) a modified full-cost approach should be adopted in which costs of prospecting, acquisition, exploration, and development in an area of interest where proven reserves are discovered would be capitalized as the cost of discovering and developing the reserves found in that area of interest, subject to a discounted cash flow ceiling, and similar costs in an area of interest where no reserves were found would be written off; (3) the Board should not impose successful-efforts accounting upon the industry without having provided conceptual support for the superiority of that method; (4) the arguments used by the Board are inconsistent and unsupported.[77]

The SEC's relationship with the FASB was clarified in 1973 by SEC *Accounting Series Release No. 150*, which stated that "principles, standards and practices promulgated by the FASB will be considered by the Commission as having substantial authoritative support, and those contrary to such FASB promulgations will be considered to have no such support." It also stated that "the Commission will continue to identify areas where investor information needs exist and will determine the appropriate methods of disclosure to meet these needs." This constitutes an endorsement of the FASB with some reservations in the sense that the SEC has not delegated any of its authority, or given up any right to reject, modify, or supersede FASB pronouncements through its own rulemaking procedures. In fact, prior to the creation of the FASB, the SEC had issued over 200 Accounting Series Releases on accounting, auditing, and financial matters, some of which have been in conflict with, or in fact amended or superseded, standards set by the standard-setting bodies.[78]

In the case of oil and gas accounting, the SEC, by *Securities Act Release No. 5801*, left it to the FASB to enact standards for producers of oil and gas. However, following the issuance of the exposure draft on oil and gas accounting by the FASB, the SEC issued in late 1977 two disclosure proposals (Release No. 33–5877 and No. 33–5878), that in retrospect clearly indicated a strong interest in a different approach to oil and gas accounting. In brief, the release proposes the reporting of the quantities of estimated proved reserves and the present value of future net revenues from their production. The release points out that "the proposed disclosures cannot be described as replacement cost information; however, they would provide information on the differences between the historical costs associated with proved oil and gas reserves shown in the financial statements and the future net revenues to be derived from these reserves."

In the case of the AICPA, the accounting profession relationship with the FASB was clarified by Rule 203 of the AICPA's Code of Professional Ethics, which holds that a member of the AICPA may not express

an opinion that financial statements are presented fairly in conformity
with generally accepted accounting principles if the statements depart
from an FASB statement or interpretation or an APB Opinion or Accounting Research Bulletin, unless he or she can demonstrate that, due
to unusual circumstance, the financial statements would be otherwise
misleading. Similar to ASR No. 150, Rule 203 constitutes an endorsement of the FASB with some reservations by recognizing that, in unusual
circumstances, literal compliance with presumptively binding, generally
accepted accounting principles issued by a recognized standard-setting
body may not always ensure that financial statements will be presented
fairly. This reflects the different positions adopted within the accounting
profession with regard to oil and gas accounting in particular and standard setting by the FASB in general. Hence, prior to the creation of the
FASB, the AICPA published ARS No. 11 in 1969 on successful-efforts
costing method without endorsing it. After the issuance of the exposure
draft the reactions were mixed. A study of the impact of the switch to
successful-efforts method by 36 full-cost companies by Touche Ross and
Co. showed (1) a reduction of earnings by an average of 20%; (2) a
reduction of the carrying values of oil and gas properties by an average
of 30%; and (3) a reduction of shareholders' equity by an average of
16%.[79] In general most influential CPA firms favor postponing decisions
until a conceptual framework is agreed upon. For example, Arthur Andersen & Co. says "the glaring need of the FASB for a conceptual
framework based on sound objectives of financial statements to furnish
guidelines in soiling problems is becoming more apparent today."[80]
Price Waterhouse & Co, states, "but what we didn't have then, we don't
have now, and desperately need, is a coherent framework of accounting
and reporting fastened firmly to a clear set of agreed objectives of financial statements."[81]

Other regulatory agencies have adopted federal accounting practices
to FASB pronouncements. Both the Interstate Commerce Commission
(ICC) and the Civil Aeronautic Board (CAB) have started incorporating
FASB statements and APB opinions in their uniform systems of accounts. For example, both announced their intentions to incorporate the
provisions of FASB No. 13 on lease transactions. In the case of oil and
gas accounting, some regulatory agencies and the FASB did not see eye
to eye. First, prior to the creation of the FASB, the Federal Power Commission supported full-cost accounting with order 440. Second, after the
issuance of the exposure draft by the FASB, the reactions of the regulatory agencies were mixed. The Justice Department requested the SEC

not to adopt a uniform standard of accounting for oil and gas producers until the SEC had established the impact of a possible change. In their letter to the SEC dated February 27, 1978, the Department of Justice noted the following broad anticompetitive effects that may result from impairing the access of full-cost firms to the capital markets:

- Exploration companies would be disadvantaged in their search for equity capital in the marketplace.

- Small, integrated companies would be placed at a greater disadvantage because exploration accounts for a large proportion of their total expenses.

- Entry into or expansion within the exploration market would be made more difficult when it became evident that a company beginning exploratory operations might need to sustain an extended period of loss on its balance sheets.

The Federal Trade Commission (FTC) adopted a similar position, arguing that competitive harm may result from the change in accounting method. Also concerned, the Department of Energy (DOE) held hearings in February 1978 on the issue.

Other commentators on positions taken by the standard-setting bodies include the industry, the investment banking firms and the companies concerned, educators, financial analysts, and the interested public in general. In the case of oil and gas their positions were mixed as evidenced by their public responses to the Board's discussion memorandum and exposure draft on oil and gas accounting.

The defenders of full-cost—such as the industry, small independent companies, Ralph Nader's Congress Watch, numerous investment banking firms, and a few academicians—argued that the successful-efforts method would reduce the ability of small firms to raise capital, reduce competition in the oil and gas industry, is not a realistic or accurate method, may produce financial statements that bear no relationship to economic logic or reality, and may lead to arbitrary manipulation by management. The following comment from Donaldson, Lufkin & Jenrette is typical of the views supporting the use of full cost:

Successful-efforts accounting will bring about a significant reduction in the reported earnings of most Full Cost exploration oriented companies and a significant increase in the volatility of such earnings. It is our contention that this combination will adversely affect investors' appraisal of these companies; this in turn will impair the companies' access to the equity capital markets and finally reduce and concentrate the exploration function as smaller independent companies either withdraw from its high risk effort to merge with larger entities more able to absorb these earnings fluctuations.[82]

The defenders and followers of successful-efforts accounting included mainly most of the international giants, including Exxon, Mobil, and Gulf, and a few academicians. The only major company using full-cost, Texaco, joined in 1976 the rank of the other majors by returning to successful-efforts accounting for all its operations. Some academicians appealed to the "efficient markets" literature to support the successful-efforts accounting. For example, Professor John Burton, former chief accountant of the SEC, made the following observations at the DOE hearings:

A number of different techniques and research designs have been used to try to isolate the market effect of alternative accounting approaches. The over-whelming preponderance of results in this research has indicated that the mar-ketplace is highly sophisticated in dealing with accounting differences and that market prices therefore adjust for these differences. Various research efforts have tested market effect when companies changed accounting principles and among companies using alternative principles and concluded in both cases that no discernible effect can be found unless the change also has tax impli-cations.

To this situation characterized by various players and various options, any position by the FASB would be accommodating some of the players. Adopting full-cost accounting would be acceptable to some of the members of the Board, the accounting firms, the members of Congress, the regulatory agencies, small companies, investment banking firms' finan-cial analysts, and other interested people, which constitute 50% of the respondents to the FASB draft. Adopting successful-efforts accounting would be acceptable to some of the members of the Board, the account-ing firms, the major oil firms in the industry, and various interested people.

The political stand chosen by the FASB was to choose the successful-efforts method. By doing so it may have attempted first to seek a compromise solution to a complex problem vis-à-vis the oil industry and companies; second, affirm the credibility of the FASB as a standard-setting body vis-à-vis the SEC and other regulatory agencies. This po-sition may show an understanding of the political process by the FASB refusing to play a minor role in those cases that the SEC and Congress consider of vital importance for the national economy. This view is echoed by Charles Horngren when he states:

Although I believe that politics is a central problem for the FASB, as it is for the APB, this does not mean that the FASB must or should be a reactive body. Indeed, it must show courage in addition to responsiveness. For example, the APB took several approaches on various issues. Sometimes it won (income tax allocation and applying Opinion No. 9 to commercial banks); sometimes it lost (the investment tax credit or retreating on its initial stance that abolished pooling of interest). But the APB was by no means the lackey of special interest. The FASB seems fearless (some would say imprudent) when it exposed its statements, Financial Reporting in Units of General Purchasing Power.[83]

Critical Evaluations

The above analysis has revealed the usefulness and some weaknesses of the use of the Allison approach to an understanding of the standard-setting decision by the FASB. The Allison approach was useful in showing that the rationale behind the decision of the FASB to adopt the successful-efforts method may be understood along various dimensions of reality and using three different conceptual models. The decision may be viewed as rational, organizational, or political. The resulting three interpretations could be, however, contradictory or complementary. For example, the political model argued for either the full-costing or the successful-efforts method. Either choice was a political stand. If the analyst views the political model as arguing for full-costing, the interpretations would be complementary. In any case, one or more interpretations may appear to dominate. In the case of oil and gas accounting, the rational and organizational interpretations appear to dominate the political model. The analyst, like this author, may be tempted to choose the political stand that corresponds to either the rational or organizational interpretations.

The above discussion points to major weaknesses of the Allison approach:

1. The first weakness may arise from the possible case where three different interpretations resulted from the three models. In fact, the three different interpretations may be the rule rather than the exception when a multitude of conflicting events preceded the decision, and the analyst

has to choose some of those events to use in each model. The choice of what is a relevant event by the analyst may influence the interpretation resulting from each model. The three interpretations could also be different due not only to the *units of analysis* but also to differences in the *level of analysis.*

The basic unit of analysis is the FASB action as a rational choice for Model I, as organizational output for Model II, and as political resultant for Model III. As admitted by Allison, Models II and III deal with aggregates, while Model I focuses on only a single actor. Consequently, the explanations of the organizational processes and political models will be by definition more elaborate and complex, with less vigor and consistency than the deductive explanation of the rational model. Moreover, the explanation of Models II and III are at a comparatively lower level. Model II, based on the previous repertoires, explains the result only in terms of similarity to previous treatments. Model III explains the result by recounting the parameters of the bargaining game without explaining what causes one player to have more power than another.

2. The second weakness exists principally in the political model. If there is no possible alternative capable of creating a consensus of acceptance between the various players, any choice is a political choice. Choosing either full-cost or successful-efforts accounting is a political choice by the FASB.

3. The third weakness exists in the data collection methodology used in the three models. It is a documentary method based on examination and analysis of the testimony, transcripts, and prepared statements of the participants. For more reliability, it may be possible, and more desirable, to augment this sort of documentary analysis with observational and interview models. In fact, Models II and III may attain a higher level of precision in their explanation if the positions and tactics of the players and the standard operating procedures were uncovered by a field study. Another approach is the idea of a cognitive map of a person's stated values and causal beliefs.[84] Applied to the FASB's decisions it consists of examining verbatim transcripts of its deliberations and deriving cognitive maps of the members of the committee according to various coding rules. Assuming verbatim transcripts may be obtained, this approach would be useful in determining the positions of each of the FASB's members. There are, however, serious limitations to the cognitive mapping approach, such as the potential for insincerity in policy decisions, the slowness of the documentary coding methods, the absence of any

types of relationships in cognitive maps other than causal or value relationships, and the lack of quantification in the relationships that are represented.[85]

4. Other weaknesses were also reported by Allison when applying the three models to explain the U.S. decision to impose a blockade in Cuba during the Cuban Missile Crisis. For example, Allison had problems in differentiating the Model II from the Model III explanation. Similarly, Chong-do Hah and Robert M. Lindquist formed the same weakness in applying the Allison's approach to the 1952 steel seizure decision by President Harry Truman.[86] They also attributed the differences in the resulting explanations not only to unit of analysis but also to differences in the level of analysis.[87]

5. Another weakness results from different analysts relying on different dimensions of reality, resulting in different interpretations—for example, a study by Cheshire and Feroz resulted in the following conclusions: "(i) The FASB Statements Nos. 5 and 13 are better explained by the rational actor model although they have elements of the organizational process model. (ii) The FASB Statements Nos. 2 and 19 are better explained by the organizational process model."[88] Exhibit 4.1 shows these interpretations are much different from those obtained in Belkaoui's study.[89]

CONCLUSIONS

The usefulness of the Allison approach rests on the ability of the analyst to determine the relevant and important dimensions of reality that influenced the final decision and the use of both documentary and observational and interview methods for the data collection. The ability to determine the most relevant events is necessary to ensure the right interpretation by each of the three conceptual models and to comprehend the relations between the various interpretations, whether they are interrelated; whether they shed light on each other; whether they are contradictory, complementary, or part of a larger synthesis; and whether one dominates the other. The additional use of observational and interview methods may help uncover the repertoires used in the organizational model and the parameters of the bargaining game used in the political model. The Allison approach is easily applicable to other standard-setting decisions. The final interpretation may rest on the additional use of observational and interview methods.

Exhibit 4.1
Summary of Model-Relevant Interpretations

Statement	Model I	Model II	Model III
	Belkaoui's Interpretations		
FASB No. 19	Explained because successful efforts method appears as consistent, value maximizing choice.	Explained because it is consistent with FASB No's 2, 5, 13.	Explained because there were interest groups opposing the FASB position.
	Interpretations of Cheshire and Feroz		
FASB No. 2	Not explained because underlying economic reality is impaired. It is not clear if usefulness as a value maximization criterion is ensured.	Explained because it is consistent with pre-established principles.	Not explained because actors did not act in an ad hoc fashion concerned only with serving interest groups.
FASB No. 5	The FASB developed criteria to ensure economic realities and value maximization.	Although explained in part, in terms of pre-established accounting policy, the consistency with the criterion of value maximization renders this standard better explained by Model I.	Same as FASB No. 2
FASB No. 13	Same as FASB No. 5	Same as FASB No. 5	Same as FASB No. 2
FASB No. 19	Same as FASB No. 2	Same as FASB No. 2	Same as FASB No. 2

Source: J. D. Cheshire and E. H. Feroz, "Allison's Models and the FASB Statements Nos. 2, 5, 13, and 19," *Journal of Business Finance and Accounting* (Spring 1989), p. 126. Reprinted with permission.

NOTES

1. Portions of this chapter have been adopted, with the permission of the editor, from Ahmed Belkaoui, "Standard Setting for Oil and Gas Accounting: An Analysis Using Allison's Approach," *Accounting and Finance* (May 1983), pp. 63–77.

2. W. T. Baxter, "Accounting Standards—Boon or Curse?" in *The Emmanuel Saxe Distinguished Lectures in Accounting 1978–1979* (New York: Bernard M. Baruch College, 1979), p. 30.

3. H. C. Edey, "Accounting Standards in the British Isles," in W. T. Baxter and Sydney Davidson, eds., *Studies in Accounting*, 3rd ed., London: Institute of Chartered Accountants of England and Wales, 1977), pp. 295–98.

4. Ibid., p. 57.

5. Ross M. Skinner, *Accounting Standards in Evolution* (Toronto: Holt, Rinehart and Winston of Canada, 1987), p. 622.

6. Robert G. Roland, "Duty, Obligation, and Responsibility in Accounting Policy Making," *Journal of Accounting and Public Policy* (Fall 1984), p. 225.

7. Anthony Tinker, "Towards a Political Economy of Accounting," *Accounting, Organizations and Society* (May 1980), pp. 147–60.

8. Anthony Tinker, "Theories of the State and State Accounting: Economic Reduction and Political Voluntarism in Accounting Regulation Theory," *Journal of Accounting and Public Policy* (Spring 1984), pp. 55–74.

9. David Cooper, Jr. and Michael J. Sherer, "The Value of Corporate Accounting Reports: Arguments for Political Economy of Accounting," *Accounting, Organizations and Society* (September 1984), p. 184.

10. Ronald Marshall, "Determining an Optimal Accounting Information System for an Undefined User," *Journal of Accounting Research* (Fall 1972), pp. 286–307.

11. K. Arrow, *Social Choice and Individual Values* (New York: Wiley, 1963).

12. Joel S. Demski, "The General Impossibility of Normative Accounting Standards," *The Accounting Review* (October 1973), pp. 718–23.

13. Ibid., pp. 721–22.

14. Joel S. Demski, "Choice Among Financial Reporting Alternatives," *The Accounting Review* (April 1974), pp. 221–32.

15. William H. Beaver, and Joel S. Demski, "The Nature of Financial Accounting Objectives: A Summary and Synthesis," *Studies on Financial Accounting Objectives*, supplement to *Journal of Accounting Research* (1974), pp. 170–87.

16. Barry E. Cushing, "On the Possibility of Optimal Accounting Principles," *The Accounting Review* (April 1977), p. 310.

17. Ibid., p. 313.

18. Michael Bromwich, "The Possibility of Partial Accounting Standards," *The Accounting Review* (April 1980), pp. 288–300.

19. R. J. Chambers, "The Possibility of a Normative Accounting Standard," *The Accounting Review* (July 1976), pp. 646–56.

20. Ibid., p. 651.

21. G. Tullock, "The General Irrelevance of the General Impossibility Theorem," *Quarterly Journal of Economics* (August 1967), pp. 256–70.

22. S. B. Johnson and D. Solomons, "Institutional Legitimacy and the FASB," *Journal of Accounting and Public Policy* (Fall 1984), pp. 165–83.

23. J. Buchanan and G. Tullock, *The Calculus of Consent: Logical Foundations of constitutional Democracy* (Ann Arbor: University of Michigan Press, 1962).

24. Johnson and Solomons, "Institutional Legitimacy and the FASB," p. 167.

25. Ibid., pp. 175–79.

26. G. J. Stigler, "The Theory of Economic Regulation," *Bell Journal of Economics* (Spring 1971), pp. 3–21.

27. R. A. Posner, "Theories of Economic Regulation," *Bell Journal of Economics* (Autumn 1974), pp. 335–58.

28. Ibid., p. 336.

29. S. Peltzman, "Toward a More General Theory of Regulation," *The Journal of Law and Economics* (August 1976), pp. 211–40.

30. George, J. Benston, "Accounting Standards in the U.S. and the U.K., Their Nature, Causes and Consequences," *Vanderbilt Law Review* (January 1975), p. 255.

31. M. E. Hussein and J. E. Ketz, "Ruling Elites of the FASB: A Study of the Big Eight," *Journal of Accounting, Auditing, and Finance* (Summer 1980), pp. 354–67.

32. N. J. Gonedes, and N. Dopuch, "Capital-Market Equilibrium, Information Production, and Selecting Accounting Techniques: Theoretical Framework and Review of Empirical Work," *Studies on Financial Accounting Objectives*, supplement to *Journal of Accounting Research* (1974), pp. 48–129.

33. R. W. Leftwich, "Market Failure Fallacies and Accounting Information," *Journal of Accounting and Economics* (December 1980), p. 200.

34. R. Ball, "Changes in Accounting Techniques and Stock Prices," *Empirical Studies in Accounting: Selected Studies*, supplement to *Journal of Accounting Research* (1972), p. 4.

35. Leftwich, "Market Failure Fallacies and Accounting Information," p. 208.

36. Homer Kripke, "World Market Forces Cause Adequate Disclosure Without SEC Mandate," in A. R. Abdel-Khalik, ed., *Government Regulation of Accounting and Information* (Gainesville: University Presses of Florida, 1980), p. 210.

37. P. R. Brown, "FASB Responsiveness to Corporate Input," *Journal of Accounting, Auditing, and Finance* (Summer 1982), p. 283.

38. Robert S. Kaplan, "Should Accounting Standards Be Set in the Public or Private Sector?" in J. W. Buckley and J. F. Weston, eds., *Regulation and the Accounting Profession* (Belmont, CA: Lifetime Learning Publications, 1980), p. 185.

39. U.S. Senate Committee on Government Operations, Subcommittee on

Reports, Accounting, and Management, *Summary of the Accounting Establishment. A Staff Study* (New York: National Association of Accountants), December 1976.

40. Kaplan, "Should Accounting Standards Be Set in the Public or Private Sector?" p. 183.

41. Ibid.

42. R. K. Elliot and W. Schuetze, "Regulation of Accounting: A Practitioner's Viewpoint," in Abdel-Khalik, ed., *Government Regulation of Accounting Information*, pp. 109–10.

43. J. W. Buckley and P. O'Sullivan, "Regulation and the Accounting Profession: What Are the Issues?" in Buckley and Weston, eds., *Regulation and the Accounting Profession*, pp. 46–48.

44. John C. Burton, "The SEC and Financial Reporting: The Sand in the Oyster," in Abdel-Khalik, ed., *Government Regulation of Accounting Information*, p. 74.

45. Ibid., pp. 79–80.

46. Ibid., p. 85.

47. Ibid., p. 80.

48. Kaplan, "Should Accounting Standards Be Set in the Public or Private Sector?" p. 187.

49. M. N. Chetkovich, "The Accounting Profession Responds to the Challenge of Regulation," in Buckley and Weston, eds., *Regulation and the Accounting Profession*, p. 148.

50. R. A. Buchholz, "Corporate Cost for Compliance with Government Regulation of Information," in Abdel-Khalik, ed., *Government Regulation of Accounting and Information*, p. 26.

51. W. Niskaven, *Bureaucracy and Representative Government* (Chicago: Aldine Atherton Press, 1971).

52. R. L. Watts, "Beauty Is in the Eye of the Beholder: A Comment on John C. Burton's 'The SEC and Financial Reporting: The Sand in the Oyster,' " in Abdel-Khalik, ed., *Government Regulation of Accounting Information*, pp. 99–100.

53. This point was suggested to me by Professor Ronald Picur, University of Illinois at Chicago.

54. David Mosso, "Regulation and the Accounting Profession: An FASB Members View," in Buckley and Weston, eds., *Regulation and the Accounting Profession*, p. 137.

55. Two other techniques—discovery value accounting and current value accounting—not presently followed by oil- and gas-producing companies have also been proposed as possible alternative treatments.

56. G. T. Allison, *Essence of a Decision: Explaining the Cuban Missile Crisis* (Boston: Little, Brown, 1971).

57. Ibid., p. 31.

58. Ibid.

59. Robert E. Field, *Accounting Research Study No. 11: Financial Reporting in the Extractive Industries* (New York: AICPA, 1969).

60. John H. Myers, *Full Cost Versus Successful-Efforts: An Empirical Approach* (New York: Petroleum Institute, 1974).

61. Federal Power Commission, *Order No. 440*, November 5, 1971, 36 F.R. 21963.

62. Financial Accounting Standards Board, *Statement of Financial Accounting Concepts No. 1: Objectives of Financial Reporting by Business Enterprises* (Stamford, CT: FASB, 1928), p. viii.

63. Financial Accounting Standards Board, *Financial Accounting Standards No. 19: Financial Accounting and Reporting by Oil and Gas Producing Companies* (Stamford, CT: FASB, 1977), p. 74.

64. Ibid., p. 75.

65. Stanley P. Porter, *Full Cost Accounting: The Problem It Poses to Extractive Industries* (New York: Arthur Young & Company, 1972), p. 6.

66. Ginsburg, Feldman, and Bress, Attorneys for Ad Hoc Committee (Petroleum Companies), *Comments on the Ad hoc Committee (Petroleum Companies) on Full Cost Accounting*, File No. S7–464, presented to the Securities and Exchange Commission, March 14, 1973.

67. Financial Accounting Standards Board, *Financial Accounting Standard No. 19.* p. 80.

68. Ibid.

69. Thomas R. Dyckman, with the cooperation of Abbie Smith, *Financial Accounting and Reporting by Oil and Gas Producing Companies: Report on the Effect of the Exposure Draft on the Returns of Oil and Gas Company Securities* (Stamford, CT: FASB, 1977).

70. D. W. Collins and W. T. Dent, "An Empirical Assessment of Stock Market Effects of the Proposed Elimination of Full Cost Accounting in the Extractive Petroleum Industry," File No. S7–715, Securities and Exchange Commission, 1978.

71. J. D. Cheshire and E. H. Feroz, "Allison's Models, and the FASB Statements Nos. 2, 5, 13, and 19," *Journal of Business Finance and Accounting* (Spring 1989), p. 120.

72. Financial Accounting Standards Board, *Financial Accounting Standards No. 2: Accounting for Research and Development Costs* (Stamford, CT: FASB, 1974).

73. Ibid., p. 42.

74. Booz-Allen and Hamilton, Inc., *Management of New Products* (New York: Booz-Allen and Hamilton, 1968), p. 12.

75. Financial Accounting Standards Board, *Financial Accounting Standard No. 13: Accounting for Leases* (Stamford, CT: FASB, 1975), p. 60.

76. Teddy L. Coe and George H. Sorter, "The FASB Has Been Using an Implicit Conceptual Framework," *The Accounting Journal* (Winter 1977–78), p. 157.

77. Financial Accounting Standards Board, *Financial Accounting Standard No. 19*, pp. 31–38.

78. Ahmed Riahi-Belkaoui, *Accounting Theory*, 3rd ed. (London: Academic Press, 1992).

79. Letter dated March 29, 1977, from Touche Ross and Co. to the Ad Hoc Committee on Full Cost Accounting.

80. Arthur Anderson & Co, "Executive News Briefs" (January 1976).

81. Price Waterhouse & Co, "Accounting Events and Techniques" (January 19, 1976).

82. Statement delivered by John Chalsty, Managing Director of Donaldson, Lufkin, & Jenrette Securities Corporation, Department of Energy Hearings, February 21, 1978.

83. Charles T. Horngren, "Setting Accounting Standards in the 1980's," in N. M. Bedford, ed., *Accountancy in the 1980's—Some Issues: Proceedings of the Arthur Young Professors' Round Table* (Champaign: University of Illinois), March 1976, pp. 30–31.

84. Robert Axelrod, *Framework for a General Theory of Cognition and Choice* (Berkeley: Institute of International Studies, 1972).

85. Ibid., p. 51.

86. Chong-Do Hah and Robert M. Lindquist, "The 1952 Steel Seizure Revisited: A Systematic Study in Presidential Decision Making," *Administrative Science Quarterly* (December 1975), pp. 587–605.

87. Ibid., p. 602.

88. Cheshire and Feroz, "Allison's Models and the FASB Statements Nos. 2, 5, 13, and 19," p. 125.

89. Belkaoui, "Standard Setting for Oil and Gas Accounting."

SELECTED READINGS

Allison, G. T. (1971). *Essence of a Decision: Explaining the Cuban Missile Crisis*. Boston: Little, Brown.

Arthur Andersen & Co. (January 1976). "Executive News Briefs."

Axelrod, Robert. (1972). *Framework for a General Theory of Cognition and Choice*. Berkeley: Institute of International Studies.

Axelrod, Robert (ed.). (1976). *Structure of a Decision: The Cognitive Maps of Political Elites*. Princeton, NJ: Princeton University Press.

Belkaoui, A. (1981). *Accounting Theory*. New York: Harcourt Brace Jovanovich.

Belkaoui, A. (May 1983). "Standard Setting for Oil and Gas Accounting: An Analysis Using Allison's Approach." *Accounting and Finance*, pp. 63–75.

Booz-Allen and Hamilton, Inc. (1968). *Management of New Products*. New York: Booz-Allen and Hamilton.

Cheshire, J. D. and E. H. Feroz. (Spring 1989). "Allison's Models and the FASB Statements Nos. 2, 5, 13, and 19." *Journal of Business Finance and Accounting*, pp. 119–30.

Coe, Teddy L. and George H. Sorter. (Winter 1977–78). "The FASB Has Been Using an Implicit Conceptual Framework." *The Accounting Journal*, pp. 152–69.

Collins, D. W. and W. T. Dent. (1978). "An Empirical Assessment of Stock Market Effects of the Proposed Elimination of Full Cost Accounting in the Extractive Petroleum Industry." File No. S7–715, Securities and Exchange Commission.

Dyckman, Thomas R., with the cooperation of Abbie Smith. (1977). *Financial Accounting and Reporting by Oil and Gas Producing Companies: Report on the Effect of the Exposure Draft on the Returns of Oil and Gas Company Securities*. Stamford, CT: Financial Accounting Standards.

Federal Power Commission. (1971). *Order No. 440*, November 5, 36 F.R. 21963.

Federal Power Commission. (1972). *Order No. 440-A*, January, 5, F.R. 603.

Field, Robert E. (1969). *Accounting Research Study No. 11: Financial Reporting in the Extractive Industries*. New York: AICPA.

Financial Accounting Standards Board. (October 1974). *Financial Accounting Standards No. 2: Accounting for Research Development Costs*. FASB.

Financial Accounting Standards Board. (November 1975). *Financial Accounting Standards No. 13: Accounting for Leases*. FASB.

Financial Accounting Standards Board. (December 1977). *Financial Accounting Standards No. 19: Financial Accounting and Reporting by Oil and Gas Producing Companies*. FASB.

Financial Accounting Standards Board. (November 1978). *Statement of Financial Accounting Concepts No. 1: Objectives of Financial Reporting by Business Enterprises*. FASB.

Ginsburg, Feldman and Bress, Attorneys for Ad Hoc Committee (Petroleum Companies). (1973). *Comments of the Ad Hoc Committee (Petroleum Companies) on Full Cost Accounting*, File No. S7–464, presented to the Securities and Exchange Commission, March 14.

Hah, Chong-Do and Robert M. Lindquist. (December 1975). "The 1952 Steel Seizure Revisited: A Systematic Study in Presidential Decision Making." *Administrative Science Quarterly*, pp. 587–605.

Horngren, Charles T. (March 1976). "Setting Accounting Standards in the

1980's." In N. M. Bedford, ed., *Accountancy in the 1980's—Some Issues: Proceedings of the Arthur Young Professors' Round Table*. Champaign: University of Illinois, pp. 30–31.

Myers, John H. (1974). *Full-Cost Versus Successful-Efforts: An Empirical Approach*. New York: Petroleum Institute.

Porter, Stanley P. (1972). *Full-Cost Accounting: The Problem It Poses to Extractive Industries*. New York: Arthur Young & Company.

Price Waterhouse & Co. (January 19, 1976). "Accounting Events and Techniques."

5
PERSPECTIVES ON ACCOUNTING RESEARCHERS AND METHODOLOGIES

The previous chapters have covered the different perspectives/visions in accounting knowledge, research, paradigms, and standard setting. They show the richness and diversity of the approaches used in the study and research of accounting topics. This richness and diversity calls for different perspectives in the methodologies to be used and different visions in the types of researchers attracted to accounting research.

ACCOUNTING KNOWLEDGE ACQUISITION

D. A. Kolb et al. proposed an interesting model of human learning,[1] portrayed in Exhibit 5.1. Basically we start acquiring knowledge through our concrete experiences. The uniqueness of some events, rituals, or phenomena lead us to increase our observations and reflections on what is happening, teaching us if we are sufficiently motivated to generate hypotheses in the form of abstract concepts and generalizations. This moves us to test the hypotheses, to understand the implications of the concepts in new situations, and in the process refine our knowledge. This is exactly the process that explains accounting knowledge acquisition, moving from particular facts (observed or discovered) to particular hypotheses (constructions of the mind) to general theories (other constructions of the mind) to general and observed or discovered laws of nature.[2] This model, however, does not make a distinction between the knowledge acquisition process (method), the methodology (dictating the method), and the epistemology (dictating the methodology). The relationships be-

Exhibit 5.1
Kolb et al.'s Model of Human Learning

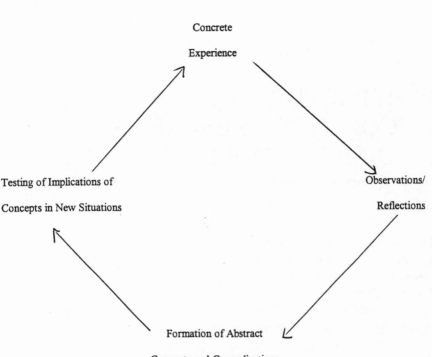

tween epistemology (why of why of how), methodology (why of how), method (how) and knowledge is shown in Exhibit 5.2. Notice that knowledge is of three types[3,4,5]: (1) knowledge-that or factual knowledge,[6] (2) knowledge-of or knowledge by acquaintance or knowledge by experience,[7] and (3) knowledge-how. The Kolb et al. model was used by Roy Payne to illustrate its role in the knowledge acquisition process.[8] It is illustrated in Exhibit 5.3. The first stage from experiencing to observing and reflecting generates a "knowledge of" or personal knowledge. The second stage from observing and reflecting to abstract theorizing generates a "knowledge-that." The methodology we use to move from abstract reasoning to testing and experimentation generates a "knowledge-how." The final stage from testing and experimentation to experiencing generates a practical "knowledge-how." It is a total process going from information, science, methodology and wisdom. Payne summarizes as follows:

Exhibit 5.2
The Relationships Between Epistemology, Methodology, Methods, and Knowledge

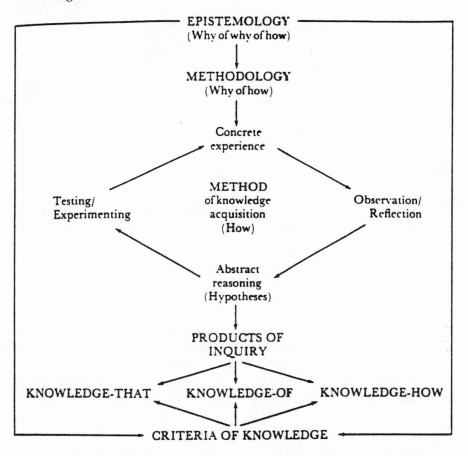

EPISTEMOLOGY
(Why of why of how)

METHODOLOGY
(Why of how)

Concrete
experience

METHOD
of knowledge
acquisition
(How)

Testing/
Experimenting

Observation/
Reflection

Abstract
reasoning
(Hypotheses)

PRODUCTS OF
INQUIRY

KNOWLEDGE-THAT   KNOWLEDGE-OF   KNOWLEDGE-HOW

CRITERIA OF KNOWLEDGE

Source: Reprinted from Roy L. Payne, "The Nature of Knowledge and Organizational Psychology," in *The Theory and Practice of Organizational Psychology*, Nigel Nicholson and Toby D. Wall, eds., p. 61, 1982, by permission of the publisher Academic Press Limited, London.

In summary, knowledge is of several types: "knowledge-how: practical" and "knowledge-of" lie within the individual. "Knowledge-that" and "knowledge-how: scientific/philosophical" are extra-individual. Since knowledge depends on individual learners, however, it is obvious that all types of knowledge are necessary to the successful working of the knowledge process. Furthermore, each type of knowledge has a different time-orientation reflecting its different roles in the knowledge process.[9]

Exhibit 5.3
Forms of Knowledge and the Learning Cycle

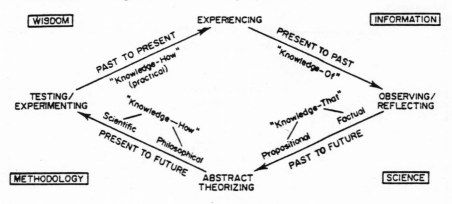

Source: Reprinted from Roy L. Payne, "The Nature of Knowledge and Organizational Psychology," in *The Theory and Practice of Organizational Psychology*, Nigel Nicholson and Toby D. Wall, eds., p. 43, 1982, by permission of the publisher Academic Press Limited, London.

CLASSIFICATION OF ACCOUNTING RESEARCHERS

The variety of knowledge and the knowledge acquisition process lead to the need to classify scientists in general and accounting researchers in particular. Various frameworks are possible for the classification of researchers in general, including the typologies of Liam Hudson,[10] Gerald Gordon,[11] Mitroff's survey of the Apollo Scientists,[12,13] Abraham Maslow,[14] and C. G. Jung.[15] It is, however, the typology of C. G. Jung that seems the most useful in classifying scientist in general[16] and accounting researchers in particular.[17] Basically, Jung classified individuals depending on sensation or intuition, and the way they reach decisions by thinking or feeling. Here are the definitions of these components of the Jungian dimensions:

Sensation involves receiving information through the senses, focusing on detail, emphasizing the here and now and the practical. Intuition, in contrast, involves input of information through the imagination, emphasizing the whole on gestalt, dwelling in idealism, in hypothetical possibilities, and taking an interest in the long term. . . . Thinking is concerned with the use of reasoning which is impersonal and formal to develop explanations in scientific, technical and theoretical terms. Feeling, on the other hand, relates to the reaching of decisions on the

Exhibit 5.4
Jungian's Typology of Researchers

Thinking

Sensing-Thinking	Thinking-Intuition
Or	Or
AbstractScientist	Conceptual Theorist

Sensing ——————————————————————— Intuition

Sensing-Feeling	Feeling-Intuition
Or	Or
Particular Humanist	Conceptual Humanist

Feeling

basis of highly value judgements and focusing on human values, moral and ethical issues.[18]

The combination of the two dimensions as shown in Exhibit 5.4 results in four personality types: (1) sensing-thinking (STs), (2) sensing-feeling (SFs), (3) feeling-intuition (IFs); and (4) thinking-intuition (ITs). This typology was used by I. I. Mitroff and R. H. Kilman[19] to produce a classification of researchers: The Abstract Scientist (AS), the Conceptual Theorist (CT), the Conceptual Humanist (CH), and the Particular Humanist (PH).

The Analytical Scientist, a sensing-thinking person, is motivated by the conduct of inquiry along a precise methodology and logic, with a focus on certainty, accuracy, and reliability, and a reliance on a simple, well-defined consistent paradigm. As stated by Mitroff and Kilman:

To know is to be certain about something. Certainty is defined by the ability to "phrase" or enumerate the components of an object, event, person, or situation in a precise, accurate, and reliable fashion. Therefore knowledge is synonymous with precision, accuracy, and reliability. Any endeavor that cannot be subjected to this formula or line of reasoning is either suppressed, devalued, or set aside as not worth knowing or capable of being known.[20]

The Conceptual Theorist, a thinking-intuition person, attempts to generate multiple explanations or hypotheses for phenomena with a focus on discovery rather than testing. As stated by Mitroff and Kilman:

Whereas the AS attempts to find the single schema that best represents the world, the CT is interested in exploring, creating, and inventing multiple possible and hypothetical representations of the world—even hypothetical worlds themselves. Further, the CT's emphasis is on the large-scale differences between these different representations rather than the details of any single schema. A potential danger for the AS is getting bogged down in infinite details; a potential danger for the CT is ignoring them altogether for the sake of comprehensiveness. ASs tend to suffer from "hardening of the categories"; CTs tend to suffer from "loosening of the wholes."[21]

The Particular Humanist, a sensing-feeling person, is concerned with the uniqueness of particular individual human beings. Everyone is a unique means rather than an abstract, theoretical end.

The Conceptual Humanist, an intuition-feeling person, focuses on human welfare, directing his or her personal conceptual inquiry toward the general human good.

IDEOGRAPHY VERSUS NOMOTHESIS

The widely accepted view of the role of accounting research is that it functions to "establish general laws covering the behavior of empirical events or objects with which the science is concerned, and thereby enable us to connect together our knowledge of separately known events and to make reliable predictions of events yet unknown."[22]

To accomplish the above function, the natural science model, including careful sampling, accurate measurement, and good design and analysis of theory-supported hypotheses, is generally adopted as the model supporting good research.[23] This now has met with objection, leading to the ideographic versus nomothetic methodology debate. The distinction between the two methodologies was first made by Gordon Allport as follows:

The nomothesis approach . . . seeks only laws and employs only those procedures admitted by the exact science. Psychology in the main has been striving to make itself a completely nomothetic discipline. The ideographic sciences . . . endeavor to understand some particular event in nature or in society. A psychology of individuality would be essentially ideographic.[24]

The debate persisted over the years, sometimes with other labels such as "qualitative versus quantitative research" or "inquiry from the inside versus inquiry from the outside" or "subjective versus objective research." The difference between nomothesis and ideography stems from differences in the underlying assumptions of social science knowledge. The subjective approach to social science features a nominalism assumption for ontology, an antipositivism assumption for epistemology, a voluntarism assumption of human nature, and, finally, an ideographic assumption for methodology. However, the objective approach features a realistic ontology, a positivist epistemology deterministic assumption of human nature, and nomothetic methodology.[25] In fact, Gibson Burrell and Gareth Morgan gave an exhaustive definition of both nomothesis and ideography. The ideographic approach

is based on the view that one can only understand the social world by obtaining first-hand knowledge of the subject under investigation. It thus places considerable stress upon getting close to one's subject and . . . emphasizes the analysis in the subjective accounts which one generates by "getting inside" situations and involving oneself in the everyday flow of life—the detailed analysis of the insights generated by such encounters with one's subject and the insights revealed in impressionistic accounts found in diaries, biographies and journalistic records.[26]

On the other hand, the nomothetic approach is

basing research protocol and technique. It is epitomized in the approach and methods employed in the natural sciences. . . . It is preoccupied with the construction of scientific tests and the use of quantitative techniques for the analysis of data. Surveys, questionnaires, personality tests and standardized research instruments of all kinds are prominent among the tools which comprise nomothetic methodology.[27]

The approach—nomothesis versus ideography or inquiry from the outside versus inquiry from the inside—differs in terms of the mode of inquiry, the type of organizational action, the type of organizational inquiry, and the role of the researcher as shown in Exhibit 5.5, and in terms of a number of analytic dimensions as shown in Exhibit 5.6.[28] One noticeable difference in Exhibit 5.6 is associated with different types of knowledge. The ideographic method is interested in the knowledge of the particular as a condition for praxis, which is "a knowledge of how to act appropriately in a variety of particular situations."[29] The nomothetic method is interested in the development of universal knowledge theoria.[30]

The difference between the two modes of inquiry is best translated in other languages by the use of two separate verbs to distinguish the two ways of knowing: knowledge about and acquaintance with the French use *savoir* and *connaitre*; the Germans use *wissen* and *kennen*, in Latin it is *scrire* and *nosere*.

Although both approaches have been debated in the literature, it is not an exaggeration to state that nomothesis has dominated accounting research with its search for general laws, universal variables, and a large number of subjects. The concern has been for methodological precision, rigor, and credibility, even if often irrelevant to the reality of organizations and accounting. Accounting researchers should pay attention to more objections raised against natural science in particular and nomothesis in general. For example, Orlando Behling raised five key objections to the use of the natural science model used in social science research and applicable to accounting research, namely:

1. *Uniqueness*. Each organization, group, and person differs to some degree from all others; the development of precise general laws in organizational behavior and organization theory is thus impossible.

2. *Instability*. The phenomena of interest to researchers in organizational behavior and organization theory are transitory. Not only do the "facts" of social events change with time, but the "laws" governing them change as well. Natural science research is poorly equipped to capture these fleeting phenomena.

3. *Sensitivity*. Unlike chemical compounds and other things of interest to natural science researchers, the people who make up organizations, and thus orga-

Exhibit 5.5
Alternative Modes of Inquiry

| Mode | Primary Purpose of Knowledge-Yielding Activity | | Role of Researcher |
	Organizational action	Organizational inquiry	
From the Inside	Coping	Situational learning	Organizational actor
	Action taking	Action research	
	Managing	Clinical practice	Participant observer
	Surviving	Case research	Unobtrusive observer
			Empiricist
	Organizational design and engineering	Traditional positivistic science	Data analyst
	Controlled experimentation		Rationalistic model builder
From the Outside	Social Technolgy		

Source: R. Evered and M. R. Louis, "Alternative Perspectives in the Organizational Sciences: Inquiry from the Inside and Inquiry from the Outside," *Academy of Management Review* (June 6, 1981), p. 388. Reprinted with permission.

Exhibit 5.6
Differences Between the Two Modes of Inquiry

		MODE OF INQUIRY	
Dimension of Difference	From the Outside		From the Inside
Researcher's relationship to setting	Detachment, neutrality	- - - - - - →	"Being there," immersion
Validation basis	Measurement and logic	- - - - - - →	Experiential
Researcher's role	Onlooker	- - - - - - →	Actor
Source of Categories	A priori	- - - - - - →	Interactively emergent
Aim of inquiry	Universality and Generalizability	- - - - - - →	Situational relevance
Type of knowledge acquired	Universal, nomothetic: theoria	- - - - - - →	Particular, ideographic: praxis
Nature of data and meaning	Factual, context free	- - - - - - →	Interpreted, contextually embedded

Source: R. Evered and M. R. Louis, "Alternative Perspectives in the Organizational Sciences: Inquiry from the Inside and Inquiry from the Outside," *Academy of Management Review* (June 6, 1981), p. 389. Reprinted with permission.

nizations themselves, may behave differently if they become aware of research hypotheses about them.

4. *Lack of Realism.* Manipulating and controlling variables in organizational research change the phenomena under study. Researchers thus cannot generalize from their studies because the phenomena observed inevitably differ from their real world counterparts.

5. *Epistemological differences.* Although understanding cause and effect through natural science research is an appropriate way of "knowing" about physical phenomena, a different kind of "knowledge" not tapped by this approach is more important in organizational behavior and organizational theory.[31]

F. T. Luthans and T. R. Davis questioned the "sameness assumption" implied by nomothesis—namely, the selective examination of many subjects under the theoretical assumption that there are more similarities than differences among individuals.[32] Based on an interactive theoretic assumption of behavior-person-environment, of real people interacting in real organizations, ideography is suggested as a useful approach using intensive single-case experimental designs and direct observational measures.[33] Luthans and Davis stated:

Central to an ideographic approach to interactive organizational behavior studies in a natural setting that intends to examine and make conclusions and test specific hypotheses are intensive single case experimental designs and direct methods such as systematic participant observations. When understood and on close examination, it turns out that these designs and methods hold up as well (and some ideographic researchers would argue better) to the same evaluative criteria for scientific research that currently are being used by nomothetically-based researchers.[34]

Among the qualitative or ideographic methodologies used, ethnography and phenomenology have gained a solid place. *Ethnography* is used by anthropologists immersing themselves in other people's realities. It has reached the level of paradigm:

Paradigmatic ethnography begins when the observer, trained in or familiar with the anthropological approach, gets off the boat, train, plane, subway or bus prepared for a lengthy stay with a suitcase full of blank notebooks, a tape recorder, and a camera. Paradigmatic ethnography ends when the masses of data that have been recorded, filed, stored, checked, and rechecked are organized according to one of several interpretive styles and published for a scholarly or general audience.[35]

Accounting researchers interested in the ethnographic method would have to have a lengthy, continuous firsthand involvement in the organizational setting under study. They would require field observations to examine the deep structure as well as the surface behavior of those in it. As suggested by John Van Maanen, they would need to (1) separate the first-order concepts or facts of an ethnographic investigation and second-order concepts or theories used by the analyst to organize and explain these facts; (2) distinguish between presentational data that document "the running stream of spontaneous conversations and activities engaged in and observed by the ethnographer while in the field" and presentational data that "concern those appearances that informants strive to maintain (or enhance) in the eyes of the field worker, outsiders and strangers in general work colleagues, close and intimate associates, and to varying degrees themselves"; and (3) continuously assess the believability of the talk-based information to uncover lies, areas of ignorance, and the various taken-for-granted assumptions.[36]

Phenomenology goes beyond participant observation and ethnography by emphasizing the search for reality as it is "given" in the structure of consciousness universal to humankind. Herbert Spiegelberg described the following seven steps in phenomenology to guide the researcher:

1. To investigate particular phenomena
2. To investigate general essences
3. To grasp essential relationships among essences
4. To watch modes of appearing
5. To watch the constitution of phenomena in consciousness
6. To suspend belief in the existence of phenomena
7. To interpret the meaning of phenomena[37]

Although the debate of ideography versus nomothesis will go on in various social science literatures, there is an established school of thought that recommends the use of multiple methods. It is generally described as one of convergent methodology, multimethod/multitrait, convergent validation, or what has been called "triangulation."[38] In fact, the originator of the debate, Allport, proposed that the ideographic and nomothetic methods were "overlapping and contributing to one another."[39] The use of both methods can (1) lead to more confidence in the results,

(2) help to uncover the deviant or off-quadrant dimension of a phenomenon, (3) lead to a synthesis or integration of theories, and (4) serve as a critical test.[40]

A thread linking all of these benefits is the important part played by qualitative method in triangulation. The research is likely to sustain a profitable closeness to situation which allows greater sensitivity to the multiple sources of data. Qualitative data and analysis function as the glue that cements the interpretation of multi-method results. In one respect, qualitative data are used as a critical counter point to quantitative method. In another respect, the analysis benefits from the perceptions drawn from personal experiences and first-hand observations. Thus enters the artful researcher who uses the qualitative data to enrich and enlighten the portrait.[41]

What all of this implies for research practice is an eventual choice between the following three options:[42]

1. Pursue both nomothetic and ideographic research and then aggregate.
2. Alternate between both nomothetic and ideographic research, running back and forth between the two methods to capitalize on the strengths of one method in certain cases and overcome the deficiencies of the other method in some cases.
3. Develop a new science described eloquently as follows: "The new science (human action science) that is gradually emerging is likely to be more actor based, experientially rooted, praxis-oriented, and self-reflective than the current image of (positivistic, objective) science. It is likely to incorporate both the American 'pragmatic' thinking of Pierce, James, Dewey, and Mead and the German 'critical' thinking of Marx, Dilthey, Husserl, Weber, Heidegger, Gadamer, and Habermas. It will probably develop for the inside and bridge toward the precision and generalizability of inquiry from the outside.[43]

CONCLUSION

This chapter elaborated on the different visions in accounting knowledge acquisition, accounting methodologies, and accounting researchers. Visions in accounting knowledge acquisition differentiated between the three types of knowledge: (1) knowledge-that, (2) knowledge-of, and (3) knowledge-how. Visions in accounting researchers differentiated between four types of researchers: (1) the Conceptual Theorist, (2) the Conceptual Humanist, (3) the Abstract Scientist, and (4) the Particular Humanist. Visions in accounting methodologies differentiated between the ideography and nomothesis approaches.

NOTES

1. D. A. Kolb, I. M. Rubin, and J. M. McIntyre, *Organizational Psychology: An Experimental Approach* (Englewood Cliffs, NJ: Prentice-Hall, 1974).

2. Roy L. Payne, "The Nature of Knowledge and Organizational Psychology," in *The Theory and Practice of Organizational Psychology*, eds. Nigel Nicholson and Toby D. Wall (London: Academic Press, 1982), pp. 37–67.

3. D. Pears, *What Is Knowledge?* (New York: Harper and Row, 1971).

4. D. W. Hamlyn, *The Theory of Knowledge* (London: Macmillan, 1971).

5. J. Hospers, *An Introduction to Philosophical Analysis* (Englewood Cliffs, NJ: Prentice-Hall, 1967).

6. D. Phillips, *Abandoning Method* (San Francisco: Jossey-Bass, 1973).

7. B. Russell, *The Problems of Philosophy* (London: Butterworth, 1912).

8. Payne, "The Nature of Knowledge and Organizational Psychology."

9. Ibid., p. 46.

10. L. Hudson, *Contrary Imaginations* (New York: Scholer Books, 1966).

11. G. Gordon, "A Contingency Model for the Design of Problem Solving Research Programs: A Perspective or Diffusion Research," *Milbank Memorial Fund Quarterly* (Spring 1974), pp. 185–220.

12. I. I. Mitroff, "Norms and Counter-Norms in a Select Group of the Apollo Moon Scientists: A Case Study of the Ambivalence of Scientist," *American Sociological Review* (1973–74), pp. 579–95.

13. I. I. Mitroff, *The Subjective Side of Science: An Inquiry into the Psychology of the Apollo Moon Scientists* (Amsterdam: Elsevier, 1974).

14. A. H. Maslow, *The Psychology of Science* (New York: Harper & Row, 1966).

15. C. G. Jung, *Collected Works, Vol. 6, Psychological Types* (Princeton, NJ: Princeton University Press, 1971).

16. I. I. Mitroff, and R. H. Kilman, *Methodological Approaches to Social Science* (San Francisco: Jossey-Bass, 1978).

17. Nandan Choudhury, "Starting Out in Management Accounting Research," *Accounting and Business Research* (Summer 1967), pp. 205–20.

18. Ibid., p. 206.

19. Mitroff and Kilman, *Methodological Approaches to Social Science*.

20. Ibid., p. 33.

21. Ibid., p. 68.

22. R. Braithwaite, *Scientific Explanation* (Cambridge: Cambridge University Press, 1973), p. 1.

23. T. D. Cole and D. T. Campbell, "The Design and Conduct of Quasi-Experiments and True Experiments in Field Settings," in M. D. Dunnette, ed., *Handbook of Industrial and Organizational Psychology* (Chicago: Rand McNally, 1976).

24. Gordon W. Allport, *Personality: A Psychological Interpretation* (New York: Henry Holt, 1937), p. 22.

25. G. Burrell and G. Morgan, *Sociological Paradigms and Organizational Analysis* (London: Heinemann, 1979).

26. Ibid., p. 6.

27. Ibid., pp. 6–7.

28. R. Evered and M. R. Louis, "Alternative Perspectives in the Organizational Sciences: Inquiry from the Inside and Inquiry from the Outside," *Academy of Management Review* 6 (1981), pp. 385–95.

29. Ibid., p. 390.

30. J. Habermas, *Knowledge and Human Interest* (Boston: Beacon Press, 1971).

31. Orlando Behling, "The Case for the Natural Science Model for Research in Organizational Behavior and Organizational Theory," *Academy of Management Review* 5 (1980), pp. 484–85.

32. F. Luthans and T. R. Davis, "An Ideographic Approach to Organizational Behavior Research: The Use of a Single Case Experimental Designs and Direct Measures," *Academy of Management Review* 3 (1982), p. 382.

33. Ibid., p. 380.

34. Ibid.

35. Peggy Reeves Sanday, "The Ethnographic Paradigm(s)," *Administrative Science Quarterly* (December 1979), p. 525.

36. John Van Maanen, "The Fact of Fiction in Organizational Ethnography," *Administrative Science Quarterly* (December 1979), pp. 539–50.

37. H. Spiegelberg, "The Essentials of the Phenomenological Method," in *The Phenomenological Movement: A Historical Introduction*, 2nd ed. (The Hague: Martinus Nijhoff, 1965), pp. 655–57.

38. O. T. Campbell and D. W. Fiske, "Convergent and Discriminant Validation by the Multitrait-Multimethod Matrix," *Psychological Bulletin* 56 (1959), pp. 81–105.

39. Allport, *Personality*, p. 22.

40. Todd D. Jick, "Rising Qualitative and Quantitative Methods: Triangulation in Action," *Administrative Science Quarterly* (December 1979), p. 605.

41. Ibid., p. 609.

42. Evered and Louis, "Alternative Perspectives in the Organizational Sciences," pp. 392–94.

43. Ibid., p. 394.

SELECTED READINGS

Beck, S. J. (1953). "The Science of Personality: Nomothetic or Ideographic?" *Psychological Review* 60, pp. 353–59.

Behling, Orlando. (1980). "The Case for the Natural Science Model for Research in Organizational Behavior and Organizational Theory." *Academy of Management Review* 5, pp. 483–90.

Behling, Orlando. (1979). "Functionalism as a Base for Midrange Theory in Organizational Behavior and Organization Theory." In C. C. Pinder and L. Moore, eds., *Middle Range Theory and Study of Organization*. Leiden: Martinus Nijhoff.

Behling, O. and M. Shapiro. (1979). "Motivation Theory: Source of the Solution or Part of the Problem?" *Business Horizons* 7, pp. 59–66.

Bernstein, R. J. (1971). *Praxis and Action*. Philadelphia: University of Pennsylvania Press.

Bernstein, R. J. (1977). "Why Hegel Now?" *Review of Metaphysics* 31, pp. 29–60.

Boehm, V. R. (1980). "Research in the Real World—A Conceptual Model." *Personal Psychology* 33.

Burtt, E. A. (1943). "The Status of 'World Hypotheses.' " *Philosophical Review* 52, pp. 590–601.

Hamlyn, D. W. (1971). *The Theory of Knowledge*. London: Macmillan.

Hospers, J. (1967). *An Introduction to Philosophical Analysis*. Englewood Cliffs, NJ: Prentice-Hall.

Kolb, D. A., I. M. Rubin, and J. M. McIntyre. (1974). *Organizational Psychology: An Experimental Approach*. Englewood Cliffs, NJ: Prentice-Hall.

Kuhn, T. S. (1962). *The Structure of Scientific Revolutions*. Chicago: University of Chicago Press.

Payne, Roy L. (1982). "The Nature of Knowledge and Organizational Psychology." In Nigel Nicholson and Toby D. Wall, eds., *The Theory and Practice of Organizational Psychology*. London: Academic Press, pp. 32–67.

Pears, D. (1971). *What Is Knowledge?* New York: Harper and Row.

Pepper, S. C. (1966). *Concept and Quality*. Chicago: Open Court.

Pepper, S. C. (1942). *World Hypotheses: A Study in Evidence*. Berkeley: University of California Press.

Rescher, N. (1977). *Methodological Pragmatism: A Systems-Theoretic Approach to the Theory of Knowledge*. Oxford: Basil Blackwell.

Rozeboom, W. W. (1972). "Problems in the Psycho-Philosophy of Knowledge." In J. R. Royce and W. W. Rozeboom, eds., *The Psychology of Knowledge*. New York: Gordon and Breach.

Russell, B. (1912). *The Problems of Philosophy*. London: Butterworth.

Weick, K. E. (1974). "Middle-Range Theories of Social Systems." *Behavioral Science* 19, pp. 357–67.

6
PERSPECTIVES ON THE SOCIOLOGY OF ACADEMIC ACCOUNTANTS

Searching for professional values was a main concern of accountants in the last decade.[1] Several major projects were undertaken to find the objectives of accounting and financial reporting.[2,3,4] Similarly, academic accountants have shown a heightened awareness of the role of values in their professional activities. The American Accounting Association established a committee to examine academic independence.[5] A code of research ethics has been suggested.[6] "Invisible colleges" have been noticed.[7] These seemingly isolated instances reflect an underlying interest in the sociology of academic accountants.

At issue is whether accounting is "value free." While accounting practice is concerned with being "free from bias," accounting research is concerned with being "scientific." In both cases, accountants profess to practice their craft free of personal values. Is this possible? Accounting practitioners and researchers have personal views and professional commitments about the kinds of issues to solve or study. It is plausible that personal values influence the choice of specific social or economic issues to investigate and the interpretation of results. Even physical scientists' work is affected by their personal commitments and values.[8] Because the influence of personal values may conflict with the ideal of scientific neutrality in accounting research, it is important to study the dimensions of professional value judgments of academic accounts. This chapter reports the results of such an empirical investigation.

RATIONALE

Value Investigation and Sociology of Accounting

The study of the professional value and belief systems of academic accountants is based on the rationale for studying values in general. Values are determinants of attitude and behavior. Because a person possesses considerably fewer values than attitudes, values are a more economical tool with which to study persons, groups, nations, and cultures.[9,10] C. Morris suggests that the term *axiology* (the study of values) refers to "the study of preferential behavior."[11] A value may be either positive or negative and may be directed to all kinds of objects and situations. An individual shows positive preferential behavior to an object or situation (a complex of objects, including their properties) if he or she acts to maintain its presence or to create it if it does not exist. Preferential behavior, therefore, manifests itself in a continuous sequence of acceptance or rejection of various objects or situations in life. An objective of scientific inquiry of value initially is to ascertain this preferential behavior.

A study of the value and belief system of accounting academicians will help us understand their attitudes and preferential behavior, particularly regarding the various aspects of the accounting discipline and profession. Our intent is to contribute toward a sociology of academic accountants, which has emerged in response to two factors. First, the development of accounting has been marked by persistent conflicts over different styles and areas of inquiry—the right issues to be examined, the right methodology to be used, the schism between accounting research and practice, the appropriate reference groups, and the professional versus disciplinary perspectives on accounting. These conflicts are probably rooted in the diverse value premises academic accountants make regarding the proper mission, scope, and conduct of accounting research. A clear understanding of these conflicts requires a study of the occupational ideologies of accounting academicians. Second, social processes in the accounting discipline affect the social organization and intellectual outputs of accounting academicians. These social processes are shaped by some significant developments over the years. There have been significant increases in the number of academic accountants and doctoral programs in accounting. Academic accountants are remunerated better than before and better than other academicians on the average. The professional organization of academic accountants has strengthened and diversified. Academic accountants are using diverse methodologies and doing more applied and commissioned research, as the sources and volume of research funds have increased.

The professional beliefs and values of accounting academicians permeate the social processes and conflicts just cited. Studying them as a first step toward a sociology of accounting will help us to explain academic ascendants' preferential behavior and to predict future developments in accounting.

Professional Value System of Academic Accountants

The professional value system of academic accountants is a conceptual net encompassing not only their definitions of accounting—what it is, what it has been and will be, and what it should be—but also the academic accountants' implicit and basic assumptions concerning their discipline as a science and occupation. As will be discussed, an analysis of the relevant literature has revealed nine major value dimensions compatible with this interpretation.

Worldviews. Successive committees of the American Accounting Association examined the intellectual achievements and failures of the profession.[12,13,14] The latest attempt observed the discontinuities in the intellectual history of accounting. The committee attributed the existence of multiple theories of financial accounting (i.e., true income, decision usefulness, information economics) to the different worldviews held by accounting researchers. The cleavages are, in the committee's opinion, so wide that "theory closure" would not be possible. This led Belkaoui to characterize accounting as a "multipleparadigm science."[15]

We hypothesize that diverse accounting paradigms are due to differences in fundamental metaphorical assumptions accounting theorists hold about human behavior. Social philosophers and scientists similarly disagree as to whether human behavior is simple or complex, predictable or unpredictable, rational or irrational, whether the social and economic system is basically stable or unstable. They also differ in their orientations toward social and economic changes, and attitudes toward deliberate interventions to solve societal problems.[16] Value assumptions have exerted a profound influence on accounting theories concerning, for example, management planning and control,[17] the social and economic environment of accounting,[18] social change,[19,20] and the premise of self-interest underlying agency theory.[21] Because accounting information has the potential, and indeed is intended, to influence human behavior, it is important to examine accounting theorists' basic assumptions regarding human behavior.

Pure Accounting Theory. The importance and the role of pure theory in guiding the development of accounting practice have been heatedly debated. The academic accounting profession seemed troubled by its dual role as an aspiring social science,[22,23] and as the research arm of a well-established profession.[24] Diverse approaches have aimed at solving this dilemma.[25] This dimension of the professional value system deals with the value of theory construction and verification as the proper work of the accounting researcher, the problem of codifying empirical findings, the difference between theory and research, the historical approach, the importance of ingenuity in theory, the development, and the usefulness of pure accounting theory.

Societal Role. Accountants perform an information production and dissemination function in society. In these activities, they make certain assumptions about the nature of the economic system and about the intended uses and users of accounting information. For example, one assumption regards owners, investors, and creditors as primary external users, and managers as internal users. Another is that accounting facilitates the efficient operation of the firm and the capital market. Recently, debates about broader social responsibilities of the firm have resulted in more interest in socioeconomic accounting and accountants' societal role.[26,27] For example, accountants generally work for those paying for their professional services. Do they have a social obligation to make their services available to those who cannot afford their fees?[28] These Accountants for the Public Interest (API) sharpen controversies over the societal role of accounting.[29] Similarly, one can ask whether academic accountants have a social responsibility beyond the production and dissemination of knowledge. For example, should they try to increase the effectiveness of social institutions through the application of their knowledge?

Given this increased interest in the societal role of accountants, we include societal role as a dimension in the professional value system to deal with the role of the academic accountant as an intellectual social critic, the dilemma between passively studying and actively attempting to solve social problems, and the social utility of accounting knowledge.

Scientific Method. When academic accountants progress from merely codifying existing practices to the construction of empirically verifiable propositions, scientific method becomes an increasingly important research approach. It contrasts sharply with intuition and politics as tools of inquiry.[30] "Generally accepted accounting principles" are critically examined by the academic accountant qua researcher. Experimental or quasi-experimental designs are widely adopted, and statistical literacy is a virtually universal requirement. Paradoxically, the increase in scientific sophistication has also widened the schism between the academic world and the practitioner world and the generation gap among academic accountants themselves.

Given these developments, we hypothesize that the emphasis on the scientific method is a professional value that may divide academic accountants into different camps. This value dimension treats the contrast between rigorous statistical methods, experimental and laboratory methods on the one hand, and direct observation, field research, inventiveness, and intuition on the other hand.

Value Freeness. Objectivity and neutrality are the essential characteristics of scientific investigations. This requirement poses a serious challenge to social sciences in general and accounting research in particular. Some seem to believe that by engaging in positive research, which seeks to describe the world as it is, research avoids making unsupported value judgments. This position overlooks the partisan role of the theories and theoreticians in questions of social order, conflict, and control.[31] Positive accounting theories rest on conservative ideologies and are contradicted by alternative radical approaches to accounting policies.[32] An example of the conservative ideology is the assertion that a basic function of accounting in the United States is to maintain the smooth operations of the capitalistic economic system.[33] These arguments highlight the delicate balance that accountants need to maintain between neutrality and utility, users' right to know, and the firm's duty to disclose.

The issue of value freeness increases in saliency as academic accountants are increasingly involved in the accounting policy-making process as staff members, consultants, and commissioned researchers. As president of the American Accounting Association, M. Moonitz expressed his concern over the reluctance of accounting professors to serve as expert witnesses in litigation involving CPA firms for fear of jeopardizing their financial supports.[34] One may wonder whether academic independence, value freeness, and research agendas are affected by the increased support of academic researchers by CPA firms.

Given this situation, we hypothesize that value freeness is an important part of the professional values of academic accountants. Basically it concerns the principles of ethical neutrality, value freeness as a central scientific canon, the possible biases created by external support, the relation between the value-free ideal and the autonomy of accounting researchers, and the political implications of external support for an accounting value system.

Professionalization. Academic accountants belong to the accounting profession and to the academic community. Hence they may have conflicts that arise from the differences between professionalism and disciplinarianism.[35] For example, the movement toward professional schools of accounting has created a debate on this issue.[36] Another aspect of the issue is the organization of academic accountants as a profession. The segmentation of the members of the American Accounting Association (AAA), as evidenced by the increasing number of sections and journals, has caused considerable concern.[37] This phenomenon is interpreted as an attempt by AAA members of differing persuasions and interests to conceive of themselves as distinctive professions within a profession, thus fragmenting intellectual and social unity. Academic accountants are not currently governed by a code of ethics as are members of the American Institute of CPAs. However, a code of ethics for academic accountants has received more attention. This may be interpreted as a sign of self-regulation—an ingredient of a profession.

Given these trends, we hypothesize that professionalization is an important part of the professional values of academic accountants. Basically this professional value concerns attitudes toward the social organization and control of academic accountants, the requirements for membership in accounting organizations, the adoption of a code of ethics, the issue of licensing of academic accountants, and the relation of accounting to other disciplines.

Self-Image. How do academic accountants view themselves? C. G. Carpenter and R. H. Strawser studied the job satisfaction of academic accountants.[38] Generally, there seems to be the perception that (1) accounting thought is in a state of flux;[39] (2) academic accountants feel that their research has little impact on policy and practice, and (3) accounting is increasingly relying on inputs from other mature social-science disciplines for theoretical foundations. Given this state of affairs, we hypothesize that self-image is an important part of the professional value of academic accountants. Basically this value deals with the intellectual and philosophical content of accounting, its importance to society's goals, and the way accountants are remunerated.

Criteria for Prestige. Faculty members' publications in leading academic journals have been used as the primary criteria for judging the prestige of academic departments.[40] L. A. Nikolai and J. D. Bazley devised a ranking of organization-set prestige and investigated its impact on accounting department faculties.[41] They found that 86% of the top 20 accounting departments' faculty obtained their doctoral degrees from the same group of departments, and only about 4% of doctoral graduates of non-top-20 departments occupied faculty positions in the top 20 departments. An individual academician's personal professional prestige is thus linked with that of his or her department. A related issue is the relative importance of research versus teaching for gaining prestige in general and promotion and tenure in particular, especially given the increasing trend toward professionalism examined earlier.

Given the importance of the issue, the beliefs about criteria for prestige in accounting are considered as an important part of the professional value of academic accountants. This variable deals with the importance of scholarly publications, the system of evaluating personnel on the basis of their publications, and the relative importance of research vis-à-vis teaching.

Beliefs about People and Publics. As suggested earlier, there is a schism between academic accountants and practitioners. Some of the professional values of academic accountants presented earlier may explain the schism (e.g., the criteria for prestige motivating the publication of scholarly articles, the concern for a more academic and intellectual self-image, the attempt to produce value-free research, the emphasis on the scientific method, and the concern for pure accounting theory). They set academic accountants apart from the practitioners and others. Given this situation, the beliefs about people and publics were considered an important part of the professional values of academic accountants. This variable treats academic accountants' ways of dealing with practitioners and others, and the need to communicate to a larger audience.

MEASUREMENT OF VALUES

The fundamental objective of this study was to obtain from academic accountants empirical data relative to the important general themes of their professional value system identified earlier. These general themes are regarded as hypothetical constructs, each consisting of a number of subthemes. The constructs may be operationalized by a series of value statements concerning various facets of each theme. We constructed a questionnaire of 89 items to depict 10 general themes of sociologists' value and belief system. We found the general themes and many questionnaire items to be pertinent to a study of the value and belief system of academic accountants. Accordingly, we modified J. T. Sprehe's survey instrument to be applicable to the academic accounting profession. The value statements are classified into the nine a priori clusters identified earlier (see the Appendix at the end of this chapter).

The first part of the questionnaire asks the respondents to express their agreement/disagreement, along a 7-point Likert scale, with each of the 89 value statements. To ascertain whether the general themes possess an underlying unity in the respondents' value and belief system, a factor analysis of the responses was performed. If a factor appeared whose highly loaded items were the questionnaire items that are conceptually linked to a general theme (that is, from the same a priori cluster), we would conclude that the particular general theme was obtained. In other words, a theme is an a priori conceptualization of value, whereas a factor is an empirically ascertained value.

HYPOTHESES AND METHODS OF ANALYSIS

First-Order Hypotheses

The first-order hypotheses address the question: What are the values and beliefs of academic accountants? or What are the contents of occupational ideologies of academic accountants? We are concerned with the unity of the principal themes. Given that each theme contains a group of opinion statements intended to operationalize it, the test for confirmation of a first-order hypothesis consists of a statistical analysis of questionnaire data to determine whether a group of items actually did possess the hypothesized unity. The responses to all items of the questionnaire are factor analyzed to see if a factor would appear whose most highly loaded items were the items that made up the group of items of a given theme.

There are nine main themes or a priori clusters used in this study. Consequently there are nine first-order hypotheses stipulating that the obtained factor structure would resemble the group of items selected for each of the nine general themes. We are thus using factor analysis in the confirmatory manner.

Second-Order Hypotheses

After the value dimensions were identified by factor analysis, we would then inquire into the possible relationships among them. That is,

Exhibit 6.1
Expected Interrelations Among Value Dimensions: Second-Order Hypothesis

		I	II	III	IV	V	VI	VII	VIII	IX
World views	I	1	-	+	-	-	-	+	+	+
Pure Accounting Theory	II		1	-	-	+	+	+	+	-
Societal Role	III			1	-	-	-	-	-	+
Scientific Method	IV				1	+	+	+	+	-
Value Freeness	V					1	+	+	+	-
Professionalization	VI						1	+	+	-
Self-image	VII							1	+	-
Prestige	VIII								1	-
People and Public	IX									1

are they positively or negatively correlated? Positive correlation between two value dimensions implies that they express a similar fundamental value. Negative correlation, on the other hand, suggests that they are in conflict. Exhibit 6.1 presents the expected signs of correlations between all pairs of clusters. The directions of the relations are based on the premise that there were two basic value subsystems. The first emphasizes an active societal role of academic accountants in promoting social change and relating to others external to the academic accounting profession. The second subsystem, on the contrary, stresses the internal development of academic accounting as a scientific discipline. Hence, importance is attached to the development of pure accounting theory, application of scientific method, adherence to the precept of value freeness in professional conduct, and using these attributes in projecting self-image and as criteria in bestowing prestige on individuals.

Two statistical methods were used in this study to test, respectively, the two sets of hypotheses identified earlier. First, responses to the 89 value statements were factor analyzed to discover the major dimensions of academic accountants' value system. Second, a correlation analysis was made of the salient factors to ascertain the relationships among them.

Choice of Population

The population of this study was academic accountants associated with colleges and universities in the United States. Operationally this meant those listed in the Academic Year 1981–82 Accounting Faculty Directory published by Prentice-Hall. Every fifth person in the directory was selected. Excluded were deans of business schools and faculty member of Canadian institutions.

The Questionnaire

The questionnaire has two parts. The first part includes 89 statements dealing with academic accountants' professional values, based on the nine general themes identified earlier. Respondents were requested to express, on a 7-point Likert scale, their agreement/disagreement with each of the statements, with 1 representing strongly agree and 7 strongly disagree. The second part asks for general background, educational, occupational, political, and religious types of demographic information.

The questionnaire, a cover letter, and a self-addressed envelope were mailed in mid-May 1982 to the sample of academic accountants described earlier. Two weeks later a postcard reminder was sent to the entire sample; a pledge of anonymity prevented us from identifying the nonrespondents. By July 15, 1982, the cutoff date, 252 out of 976 questionnaires or 26% were returned. Among those returned, 233, or 92%, were usable.

RESULTS

Characteristics of Population

Consideration of Nonresponse Bias. The relatively low response rate gave rise to a concern for nonresponse bias. The test for nonresponse bias is based on the established belief that late responses may be used as surrogates for nonresponses. First, early and late responses were identified by the receipt dates of questionnaires. Second, a sample of 15 questionnaires was chosen to constitute early and late sets. Third, mean response scores were calculated for each of the 89 opinion statements, and a student t test for noncorrelated samples with pooled variances was computed. The results of the t test (alpha $= .05$ or less) showed clearly that no differences existed between the early set and late set. The evidence failed to suggest the presence of nonresponse bias.

Demographic Characteristics of Respondents. The demographic characteristics of the respondents providing usable returns were as follows:

1. Age Distribution: 24% were below 35; 32% between 35 and 45; 21% between 46 and 55; 17% between 56 and 65; 3% over 65; 5% no response.
2. National Origin: 89% were born in the United States; 6% foreign born; 5% no response.
3. Educational Attainment: 34% did not hold doctorates. Among the doctoral degree holders, 35% were 1 to 5 years beyond degree date; 23% were 5 to 10 years beyond; 16% were 11 to 15 years beyond; 8% were 16 to 20 years beyond; 11% were 21 to 30 years beyond; 3% were over 30 years beyond.
4. Academic Rank Distribution: 28% were full professors; 23% associate professors; 32% assistant professors; 14% lecturers/instructors; 1% no response.
5. Institutional Affiliation: 81% with state universities or colleges; 11% with private, nonsectarian institutions; 7% with church-related institutions; 1% no response.
6. Institution Size: 1% had less than 1,000 enrollment; 11% between 1,000 and 5,000 enrollment; 21% between 5,000 and 10,000 enrollment; 66% over 10,000 enrollment; 1% no response.

First-Order Hypothesis

The data were submitted to a factor analysis. Applying the 1.0 eigenvalue criterion, the quartimax rotation produced a 7-factor solution accounting for 28.5% of the variance. Factors 1–7 accounted for 7.1%, 5.3%, 4.0%, 3.6%, 3.2%, 2.8%, and 2.5% of the variance, respectively. The variables found to load 0.30 or higher on a factor were selected as its domain (Exhibit 6.2). There was no evidence of a single general factor accounting for a large percentage of the variations in the data. Variance on each factor accounted for by items loaded on each factor ranged from 76% to 91%. Factor reliabilities using the formula suggested by J. C. Nunnally were 0.73, 0.62, 0.65, 0.67, 0.63, 0.64, and 0.65.[42]

The factors were named on the basis of the number of cluster items that loaded significantly on them and by investigating their underlying common trait. The name given to each factor corresponds to the cluster

Exhibit 6.2
Significant Factor Loadings

Factor #	Variable #	Value Statement	Loading
1	4	Academic accountants as researchers should view people merely as sources of data.	0. 57068
	86	The major justification for any accounting research endeavor is that it generates accounting theory.	0. 56921
	23	The most important aspect of any piece of research is its contribution to general theory.	0. 41630
2	1	Judgment of the scientific worth of a person is often distorted by appraisal of the number of his/her publications.	0. 52517
	60	Direct observation and intuitive insight are more fruitful for the accounting research than an emphasis on rigorous methodology.	0. 51713
	58	Accounting is a body of scientific knowledge and theory; it is not a philosophy of life.	− 0. 48002
	2	Although the laboratory method may make a study more rigorous, it is not as fruitful as field research.	0. 43607
	21	Emphasis on methodology too often diverts accounting researchers from a study of accounting to the problem of how to study accounting.	0. 35788
	25	The more readily academic accountants accept research funds, the more will their value-free ideal be undermined.	0. 35081
	27	The coming generation of academic accountants will need much more training in the use of higher mathematics.	− 0. 34195
3	30	Social science can aid both in achieving society's goals and in defining those goals.	0. 60800
	83	The academic accountant not only should think about communicating to professional colleagues but also should attempt to speak to a wider public.	0. 55944
	29	Accountants have an obligation to help society in somewhat the same way in which doctors are obliged to help their patients.	0. 55192
	85	One of the social functions of accounting is to strive to increase the effectiveness of social institutions.	0. 52442
	22	The academic accountant, like any other intellectual, has the right and duty to criticize contemporary society.	0. 44861
	56	It is impossible for the academic accountant to be fully competent without considerable knowledge of other social sciences.	0. 42120
	88	Academic accountants should strive harder to write in a way that is more widely understandable.	0. 40256
	43	It is impossible to view human behavior as a game or drama and be a serious academic accountant.	− 0. 35334
	87	Some of the most powerful theories in accounting have emerged from the study of actual problems.	0. 34808

Exhibit 6.2 (Continued)

Factor #	Variable #	Value Statement	Loading
	9	Active involvement in efforts to remedy social problems need not seriously bias an academic accountant.	0. 34457
4	75	Considering the extent of their contribution to science and society, academic accountants should be paid more.	0. 61769
	68	Accounting today deserves a more favorable public image than it has.	0. 59595
	81	There should be more formal prizes or awards available for academic accountants.	0. 57673
	35	People conduct their lives in a more rational manner than we often think.	0. 38216
	69	Modern societies could get along very well without the work of accountants.	−0. 34837
5	38	The notion is ridiculous that it will ever be necessary to license applied accounting researchers engaged in consulting on the basis of standardized examinations.	−0. 67645
	61	Accountants will eventually need to take steps toward the licensing of applied accounting researchers, much like psychology has done.	0. 65420
	37	Some code of ethics for academic accountants should be promulgated and strictly enforced.	0. 62570
	82	Academic accountants should take steps to keep unqualified persons from belonging to the American Accounting Association and calling themselves accounting educators/researchers.	0. 58757
	50	Once the American Accounting Association officially adopts a code of ethics, any members who deliberately violate the code ought to be dropped from the association.	0. 57042
	84	The worth of an academic accountant is best measured by the work of the people he/she teaches.	0. 33545
	89	Accounting research is at its best when it takes an historical approach to a problem rather than a synthetic, timeless viewpoint.	0. 31018
6	54	The problems of modern society are so complex that only planned change can be expected to solve them.	0. 65864
	42	By and large, social problems tend to correct themselves without planned intervention.	−0. 57229
	59	Philosophers have interpreted the world; the point, however, is to change it.	0. 53971
	46	Social science is really the philosophy of the twentieth century.	0. 36591
	67	Changing people is a more serious goal than just understanding them.	0. 36350

133

Exhibit 6.2 (Continued)

Factor #	Variable #	Value Statement	Loading
	8	Historical-cost accounting theory still retains great value for contemporary accounting.	− 0. 34931
	15	Accountants should try to structure social institutions so as to maximize the satisfaction of individual needs.	0. 32281
	17	Significant patterns of human behavior are too complex to be discovered by direct observation but require the use of precise measurements.	0. 32214
	28	The American Accounting Association is a learned society and any person with minimal qualifications should be allowed to join.	0. 28708
7	39	Accounting research is often best conducted if treated as a game.	0. 49844
	64	The subject matter of accounting makes it impossible to separate professional from nonprofessional values.	0. 44182
	24	As teachers, academic accountants can express their personal values to students.	0. 43201
	3	Academic accountants do not really keep separate their personal experience and their professional work.	0. 39874
	5!	Many social scientists are too prone to let foundations and government agencies determine the problems they will study.	− 0. 38466
	31	Formulating a study in such a way as to get public financial support is a violation of the professional integrity of an academic accountant.	− 0. 35852

with the highest number of variables loading significantly on the factor (Exhibit 6.3). These factors are examined next.

The first factor is named Pure Accounting Theory. This cluster did not fare well at the hands of the respondents. Only two items from Cluster II could be kept (Exhibit 6.4). Both items stress the primacy of accounting theory development as an objective of research. It suggests that Factor 1 measures a value regarding the quest for pure accounting theory.

The second factor is named Scientific Method. Basically this factor is a mixture of Cluster IV (Scientific Method) and items from Clusters VIII, VII, II, and V (Exhibit 6.5) with the exception of the items from Cluster VIII and V. Items in the other clusters connote a position on the scientific method. The three items from Cluster IV seem to downplay the role in accounting of the scientific method. Item 60 argues for direct observation

Exhibit 6.3
Summary: Observed Versus Expected Factors

Table 3.   Summary: Observed versus Expected Factors

Factor Number	Name of Factor	Most Clearly Corresponds to Cluster No.	No. of Cluster Items Appearing on Factor	No. of Other Items Appearing on Factor
1	Pure Accounting Theory	II	*2 (23,86)	*1 (4)
2	Scientific Method	IV	3 (21,17,60)	5 (1,2,25,58,65)
3	Societal Role and Beliefs about People and Publics	III	3 (22,29,85)	7 (9,30,43,56,83, 87,88)
4	Self-image	VII	4 (68,69,75,81)	1 (35)
5	Professionalization	VI	5 (37,38,50,59,67)	2 (84,89)
6	Worldviews	I	4 (42,54,59,67)	5 (8,15,17,28,46)
7	Value Freeness	V	5 (3,24,31,51,64)	1 (39)

*Numbers in parentheses refer to variable numbers.

and intuitive insight, Items 21 and 27 downplay, respectively, the emphasis on methodology and on higher mathematical training. The items from the other clusters indicate the same position on the scientific method. Item 58, through its negative loading, implies that accounting is a philosophy of life rather than a body of scientific knowledge and theory. Item 2 argues for field research over the more rigorous laboratory method. In conclusion, most of the items loaded significantly on this factor downplay the importance of the scientific method as a value of academic accountants.

The third factor is named Societal Role and Beliefs about People and Publics. Basically, the third factor is a mixture of Clusters III and IX (Exhibit 6.6). Five out of the 10 items highly loaded on this factor are from these two clusters. The other items highly loaded on this factor come from Clusters VII, VI, II, and V, and connote a position on societal role and beliefs about people and publics. They all stress an active role of the academic accountant in society by speaking to a wider audience (Item 83), in helping to achieve and define societal goals (Item 30), in accepting the obligation to help society (Item 29), in trying to increase the effectiveness of the social institutions (Item 85), in accepting the right and duty to criticize society (Item 22), in advocating better familiarity with other social sciences (Item 56), in writing in a more widely understandable way (Item 88), in a better view of human behavior (Item

Exhibit 6.4
Pure Accounting Theory (Factor 1)

Factor Loadings	Cluster No.	Item No.	Value Statement
0.57068	IX	4	Academic accountants as researchers should view people merely as sources of data.
0.56921	II	86	The major justification for any accounting research is that it generates accounting theory.
0.41630	II	23	The most important aspect of any piece of research is its contribution to general theory.

43), in linking powerful theories of accounting to actual problems (Item 87), and, finally, in advocating active involvements in efforts to remedy social problems (Item 9). These suggest that Factor 3 measures a value regarding accountants' societal role and beliefs about people and publics.

The fourth factor is named Self-Image. This cluster did fare well at the hands of the respondents. Most items highly loaded on this factor are from Cluster VII (Exhibit 6.7). They all refer to the positive aspect of the academic accountant's self-image by stressing the need for higher pay (Item 75), a more favorable public image (Item 68), more formal prizes and awards (Item 81), and the importance of the work of accountants to modern society (Item 69). They indicate the importance of self-image as a value of academic accountants.

The fifth factor is named Professionalization. Five of the seven items highly loaded on this factor are from Cluster VI (Exhibit 6.8). Remarkably, all five items had loadings of about 0.50. Interestingly, the respondents strongly favored the licensing of applied accounting researchers. Next in the order of importance were a code of ethics, and the restriction of AAA membership. There is evidence in general for a strong commitment to the idea of accounting as a profession.

The sixth factor is named Worldviews. It is a mixture of Cluster I (four out of the nine items) and other clusters (Exhibit 6.9). This result is not very surprising because Cluster I is exploratory. Fortunately, items from the other clusters connote a position on worldviews. In general, all the items seem to convey a position advocating planned change and intervention to correct social problems. The negative loading of Item 8 suggests the repudiation of the value of historical accounting.

The seventh factor is named Value Freeness. This cluster fared rather well. Five out of six items highly loaded on this factor are from Cluster

Exhibit 6.5
Scientific Method (Factor 2)

Factor Loadings	Cluster No.	Item No.	Value Statement
0.52517	VIII	1	Judgment of the scientific worth of a person is often distorted by appraisal of the number of his/her publications.
0.51713	IV	60	Direct observation and intuitive insight are more fruitful for accounting research than an emphasis on rigorous methodology.
−0.48002	VII	58	Accounting is a body of scientific knowledge and theory; it is not a philosophy of life.
0.43607	II	2	Although the laboratory method may make a study more rigorous, it is not as fruitful as field research.
0.35788	IV	21	Emphasis on methodology too often diverts accounting researchers from a study of accounting to the problem of how to study accounting.
0.35081	V	25	The more readily academic accountants accept research funds, the more will their value-free ideal be undermined.
0.34195	IV	27	The coming generation of academic accountants will need much more training in the use of higher mathematics.

V (Exhibit 6.10). It seems that academic accountants do not believe greatly in the ideal of ethical neutrality. They reject the idea that funding agencies determine research problems. Also, the respondents do not regard it as improper for academic accountants to voice their values and opinions in public and in the classroom, or impossible to separate professional from nonprofessional values. At the same time, they favor formulating research to get financial support (Item 31). Basically this factor stresses a lack of personal conformity with the value-free ideal and a willingness to be responsive to research sponsors.

Second-Order Hypothesis

The purpose of testing the second-order hypothesis was to ascertain the interrelations among the factors. Analysis of the factor intercorrelation matrix show in Exhibit 6.11 reveals the following (only significant correlation coefficients at the 0.10 level of significance are reported):

1. As expected, professionalization is positively related to the empha-

Exhibit 6.6
Societal Role and Beliefs About People and Places (Factor 3)

Factor Loadings	Cluster No.	Item No.	Value Statement
0.60800	VII	30	Social science can aid both in achieving society's goals and in defining those goals.
0.55944	IX	83	The academic accountant not only should think about communicating to his/her professional colleagues, but also should attempt to speak to a wider public.
0.55192	III	29	The accountant has an obligation to help society in somewhat the same way in which the doctor is obliged to help his/her patient.
0.52442	III	85	One of the social functions of accounting is to strive to increase the effectiveness of social institutions.
0.44861	III	22	The academic account, like any other intellectual, has the right and duty to criticize contemporary society.
0.42120	VI	56	It is impossible for the academic accountant to be fully competent without considerable knowledge of other social sciences.
0.40256	IX	88	Academic accountants should strive harder to write in a way that is more widely understandable.
− 0.35334	II	43	It is impossible to view human behavior as a game or drama and be a serious academic accountant.
0.34808	II	87	Some of the most powerful theories in accounting have emerged from the study of actual problems.
0.34457	V	9	Active involvement in efforts to remedy social problems need not seriously bias an academic accountant.

sis on developing pure accounting theory and using scientific method in accounting research. The intercorrelation between professionalization and pure accounting theory (r = .20) indicates that the desire of academic accountants to conceive of themselves as a distinctive profession aimed at adopting a code of ethics and regulating research and teaching activities of their members coincides perfectly with their position on the primacy and role of accounting theory development. The intercorrelation between professionalization and scientific method (r = .22) may indicate that the desire of academic accountants to conceive of themselves as a

Exhibit 6.7
Self-Image (Factor 4)

Factor Loadings	Cluster No.	Item No.	Value Statement
0.61769	VII	75	Considering the extent of their contribution to science and society, academic accountants should be paid more.
0.59595	VII	68	Accounting today deserves a more favorable public image than it has.
0.57673	VII	81	There should be more formal prizes or awards available for academic accountants.
0.38216	I	35	People conduct their lives in a more rational manner than we often think.
−0.34837	VII	69	Modern societies could get along very well without the work of accountants.

distinctive profession coincide with their position on the role of the scientific method. In short, both positions on development of accounting theory and scientific method complement their position on professionalization.

2. As expected, scientific method is negatively related to worldviews. The intercorrelation ($R = -.14$) indicates that the scientific method with its emphasis on rigor and defined procedure of conduct and inquiry comes in conflict with worldviews with its emphasis on metaphorical and essentially exploratory assumptions about the nature of human behavior, the need for social and economic changes, the need for social intervention, the nature of the social and economic system, and the role of sentiments and feelings in human life.

3. Contrary to our expectations, value freeness is negatively related to both scientific method and self-image. The intercorrelation between value freeness and the scientific method ($r = -.15$) indicates that, contrary to widely held a priori beliefs, personal values and preferences are interjected in the use of and/or choice of mathematical and statistical methods and logical deductive procedures of research. The intercorrelation between value freeness and self-image ($r = -.13$) seems to indicate again that the intellectual and philosophical development of accounting, its importance to society's goals, and the way it is renumerated is impregnated and/or influenced by the personal values of academic accountants.

Exhibit 6.8
Professionalization (Factor 5)

Factor Loadings	Cluster No.	Item No.	Value Statement
−0.67645	VI	38	The notion is ridiculous that it will ever be necessary to license applied accounting researchers engaged in consulting on the basis of standardized examinations.
0.65420	VI	61	Accountants will eventually need to take steps toward the licensing of applied accounting researchers, much like psychology has done.
0.62570	VI	37	Some code of ethics for academic accountants should be promulgated and strictly enforced.
0.58757	VI	82	Academic accountants should take steps to keep unqualified persons from belonging to the American Accounting Association and calling themselves accounting educators/researchers.
0.57042	VI	50	Once the American Accounting Association officially adopts a code of ethics, any members who deliberately violate the code ought to be dropped from the association.
0.33545	VIII	84	The worth of an academic accountant is best measured by the work of the people he/she teaches.
0.31018	II	89	Accounting research is at its best when it takes an historical approach to a problem rather than a synthetic, timeless viewpoint.

SUMMARY AND CONCLUSION

The main objective of this study was to explore the values and beliefs of academic accountants concerning accounting itself and the nature of the relations between these values and beliefs. To this end, nine major themes were posed to academic accountants via a survey questionnaire: (1) worldviews, (2) pure accounting theory, (3) societal role, (4) scientific method, (5) value freeness, (6) professionalization, (7) self-image, (8) criteria for prestige, and (9) beliefs about people and publics. The first-order hypotheses involved the expectation that the cluster of items operationalizing the main themes would turn out to be individual factors when the data were factor analyzed. The second-order hypotheses predicted some relationships between the variables.

The factor analysis yielded seven usable factors labeled (1) pure accounting theory, (2) scientific method, (3) societal role and beliefs about people and publics, (4) self-image, (5) professionalization, (6) world-

Exhibit 6.9
Worldviews (Factor 6)

Factor Loadings	Cluster No.	Item No.	Value Statement
0.65864	I	54	The problems of modern society are so complex that only planned change can be expected to solve them.
−0.57229	I	42	By and large, social problems tend to correct themselves without planned intervention.
0.53971	I	59	Philosophers have interpreted the world; the point, however, is to change it.
0.36591	VII	46	Social science is really the philosophy of the twentieth century.
0.36350	I	67	Changing people is a more serious goal than just understanding them.
−0.34931	II	8	Historical cost-accounting theory still retains great value for contemporary accounting.
0.32281	III	15	Accountants should try to structure social institutions so as to maximize the satisfaction of individual needs.
0.32214	IV	17	Significant patterns of human behavior are too complex to be discovered by direct observation, but require the use of precise measurements.
0.28708	VI	28	The American Accounting Association is a learned society, and any person with minimal qualifications should be allowed to join.

views, and (7) value freeness. Judging the factors by the items and their factor loading, pure accounting theory stresses the primacy of accounting theory as an objective of research (Factor 1). Factor 2, scientific method, downplayed the role and importance of the scientific method as a value of academic accountants. Societal role and beliefs about people and publics, Factor 3, stressed the active role in society of the academic accountant. Factor 4, self-image, stressed the need for a better image and rewards for academic accountants. Professionalization (Factor 5) showed a strong commitment to the idea of a profession. Factor 6, worldviews, involved a belief in planned change and intervention to correct social problems. Finally, Factor 7, value freeness, downplayed the role of ethical neutrality.

The second-order hypotheses concerning relations between factors were confirmed in three cases and disconfirmed in two cases. Two expectations were realized: (1) professionalization, together with pure accounting theory and scientific method, and (2) scientific method, together

Exhibit 6.10
Value Freeness (Factor 7)

Factor Loadings	Cluster No.	Item No.	Value Statement
0.49844	II	39	Accounting research is often best conducted if treated as a game.
0.44182	V	64	The subject matter of accounting makes it impossible to separate professional from nonprofessional values.
0.43201	V	24	As teachers, academic accountants can express their personal values to students.
0.39874	V	3	Academic accountants do not really keep separate their personal experience and their professional work.
−0.38466	V	51	Many social scientists are too prone to let foundations and government agencies determine the problems they will study.
−0.35852	V	31	Formulating a study in such a way as to get public financial support is a violation of professional integrity of an academic accountant.

Exhibit 6.11
Expected Versus Actual Relationships Among Factors

	Expected	Correlation Actual Sign	Value
Pure Accounting Theory and Professionalization	+	+	(.20)
Scientific Method and Professionalization	+	+	(.22)
Scientific Method and Worldviews	−	−	(−.14)
Scientific Method and Value Freeness	+	−	(−.15)
Self-Image and Value Freeness	+	−	(−.13)

with worldviews, constitute one constellation of beliefs and values. The expectations were not confirmed of a relationship between value freeness and scientific method and self-image.

In conclusion, our results appear to reflect the ideological conflicts facing academic accountants as expressed by their concern for theoretical development, a more active societal role, better self-image, and more professionalization, on the one hand, and the need for rigorous scientific method and ethical neutrality, on the other hand. The first set of concerns seems to predominate. Academic accountants are ambivalent about most of the values presented to them, and have difficulties in disassociating their personal values from professional values and beliefs.

NOTES

1. This entire chapter has been adapted with permission of the publisher from Ahmed Belkaoui and James L. Chan, "Professional Value System of Academic Accountants: An Empirical Inquiry," in *Advances in Public Interest Accounting*, Vol 2 (Greenwich, CT: JAI Press, 1988), pp. 1–28.

2. American Institute of Certified Public Accountants, Study Group on the Objectives of Financial Statements, *Objectives of Financial Statements* (New York: AICPA, 1974).

3. Financial Accounting Standards Board, *Objectives of Financial Reporting by Business Enterprises*, Statement of Financial Accounting Concepts No. 1 (Stamford, CT: FASB, 1978).

4. National Council in Governmental Accounting, *Objectives of Accounting and Financial Reporting by Governmental Units* (Chicago: NCGA, 1981).

5. American Accounting Association, Committee on Academic Independence, *Report of the Committee on Academic Independence of the American Accounting Association* (Sarasota, FL: AAA, 1981).

6. J. A. Hendricks and D. E. Keys, "Toward a Code of Accounting Research Ethics," paper presented at the annual meeting of the American Accounting Association (1982).

7. R. Ball and G. Forter, "Corporate Financial Reporting: A Methodological Review of Empirical Research," *Journal of Accounting Research*, Supplement (1983).

8. I. Mitroff, "Norms and Counter-Norms in a Select Group of Apollo Moon Scientists: A Case Study of the Ambivalence of Scientists," *American Sociological Review* (Fall 1974).

9. M. Rokeach, *Beliefs, Attitudes and Values* (San Francisco: Jossey-Bass, 1968).

10. M. Rokeach, "Religious Values and Social Companion," *Review of Religious Research* 32 (1969), pp. 547–59.

11. C. Morris, "The Study of Preferential Behavior," in R. Lepley, ed., *Value: A Cooperative Inquiry* (New York: Columbia University Press, 1949), pp. 211–22.

12. American Accounting Association, *Accounting and Reporting Standards for Corporate Financial Statements and Preceding Statements and Supplements* (Sarasota, FL: AAA, 1957).

13. American Accounting Association, Committee to Prepare a Statement for Basic Accounting Theory, *A Statement of Basic Accounting Theory* (Sarasota, FL: AAA, 1966).

14. American Accounting Association, Committee on Concepts and Stan-

dards for External Financial Reports, *Statement on Accounting Theory and Theory Acceptance* (Sarasota, FL: AAA, 1977).

15. A. Belkaoui, *Accounting Theory* (New York: Harcourt Brace Jovanovich, 1981).

16. J. T. Sprehe, "The Climate of Opinion in Sociology: A Study of the Professional Value and Belief Systems of Sociologists" (Unpublished Ph.D. dissertation, Washington University, 1967).

17. E. H. Caplan, "Behavioral Assumptions of Management Accounting," *The Accounting Review* (July 1966), pp. 496–509.

18. M. Moonitz, *The Basic Postulates of Accounting* (New York: AICPA, 1961).

19. C. W. Churchman, "On the Facility, Felicity, or Morality of Measuring Social Change," *The Accounting Review* (January 1971), pp. 30–35.

20. D. M. Gilling, "Accounting and Social Change," *The International Journal of Accounting* (Spring 1976), pp. 59–71.

21. M. C. Jensen and W. H. Meckling, "Theory of the Firm: Managerial Behavior, Agency Costs and Ownership Structure," *Journal of Financial Economics* (October 1976), pp. 305–60.

22. R. K. Mautz, "Accounting as a Social Science," *The Accounting Review* (1963), p. 317.

23. R. R. Sterling, *Scientific Accounting* (Lawrence, KS: Scholars Book Co., 1975).

24. J. W. Buckley, ed., *The Impact of Accounting Research on Policy and Practice* (New York: Council of Arthur Young Professors, 1981).

25. A. Belkaoui, "The Impact of the Disclosure of the Environmental Effects of Organizational Behavior of the Market," *Financial Management* (Winter 1976), pp. 26–31.

26. R. W. Estes, "Socio-Economic Accounting and External Diseconomies," *The Accounting Review* (April 1972), pp. 284–90.

27. D. J. Linowes, "Socio-economic Accounting," *The Journal of Accountancy* (November 1970), pp. 37–42.

28. M. Levy, *Accounting Goes Public* (Philadelphia: University of Pennsylvania Press, 1977).

29. C. R. Skousen, "Public Interest Accounting: A Look at the Issues," *Accounting, Organizations and Society* (February 1982), pp. 79–85.

30. D. L. Gerboth, "Research, Intuition, and Politics in Accounting Theory," *The Accounting Review* (July 1973), pp. 475–86.

31. J. L. Zimmerman, "Positive Research in Accounting," University of Rochester Working Paper AMERC 80–70 (1980).

32. A. M. Tinker, B. D. Merino, and M. D. Neimark, "The Normative Origins of Positive Theories: Ideology and Accounting Thought," *Accounting, Organizations and Society* (May 1982), pp. 167–200.

33. Wheat Committee, "Study on the Establishment of Accounting Principles: Establishing Financial Accounting Standards" (New York: AICPA, 1972).

34. M. Moonitz, "An Open Letter to All on a Matter of Independence," *Accounting Education News* (January 1979).

35. I. L. Horowitz, "Discussion: Professionalism and Disciplinarianism, Two Styles of Sociological Performance," *Philosophy of Science* (August 1964), pp. 275–81.

36. A. H. Bizzell and K. D. Larson, eds., *Schools of Accountancy: A Look at the Issues* (New York: AICPA, 1975).

37. T. Dyckman, "Presidents' Message," *Accounting Education News* (July 1982).

38. C. G. Carpenter and R. H. Strawser, "A Study of the Job Satisfaction of Academic Accountants," *The Accounting Review* (July 1971), pp. 509–18.

39. American Accounting Association, *Statement on Accounting Theory and Theory Acceptance.*

40. W. J. Andrews and P. B. McKenzie, "Leading Accounting Departments Revisited," *The Accounting Review* (January 1978), pp. 135–38.

41. L. A. Nikolai and J. D. Bazley, "The Organizational Set Prestige Ranking and Its Impact Upon Accounting Departments," *The Accounting Review* (October 1975), pp. 881–87.

42. J. C. Nunnally, *Psychometric Theory* (New York: McGraw-Hill, 1967), pp. 193–94.

SELECTED READINGS

Belkaoui, A. (1981). *Accounting Theory.* New York: Harcourt Brace Jovanovich.

Belkaoui, A. (1976). "The Impact of the Disclosure of the Environmental Effects of Organizational Behavior of the Market." *Financial Management* (Winter), pp. 26–31.

Levy, M. (1977). *Accounting Goes Public.* Philadelphia: University of Pennsylvania Press.

Morris, C. (1949). "The Study of Preferential Behavior." In R. Lepley, ed., *Value: A Cooperative Inquiry.* New York: Columbia University Press, pp. 211–22.

Rokeach, M. (1969). "Religious Values and Social Companion." *Review of Religious Research* 32, pp. 547–59.

Sprehe, J. T. (1967). "The Climate of Opinion in Sociology: A Study of the Professional Value and Belief Systems of Sociologists." Unpublished Ph.D. dissertation, Washington University.

APPENDIX: A PRIORI CLUSTERS OF VALUE STATEMENTS

I. Worldviews

7   Most people think human behavior is simpler than it really is.

13   The underlying reality in all groups is a series of more or less powerful tensions and conflicts.

34   Planned change is sometimes dangerous because of possible unanticipated consequences.

35   People conduct their lives in a more rational manner than we often think.

42   By and large, social problems tend to correct themselves without planned intervention.

47   The trouble with many people today is that they do not give enough expression to their feelings and sentiments.

54   The problems of modern society are so complex that only planned change can be expected to solve them.

55   The most basic sources of stability in any group are the beliefs and values that its members share.

59   Philosophers have interpreted the world; the point, however, is to change it.

65   Many modern social institutions are deeply unstable and tense.

67   Changing people is a more serious goal than just understanding them.

73   Human behavior, in the last analysis, is very unpredictable.

76   The unity of any group is only a matter of appearances; the underlying reality is great diversity and difference.

77   Many academic accountants underestimate the importance of rationality in human life.

80   Most people think human behavior is more complex than it really is.

II. Pure Accounting Theory

2   Although the laboratory method may make a study more rigorous, it is not as fruitful as field research.

8   Historical cost accounting theory still retains great value for contemporary accounting.

14   I would like to devote more of my time to the development of pure accounting theory.

23   The most important aspect of any piece of research is its contribution to general theory.

39   Accounting research is often best conducted if treated as a game.

41   Ingenuity in designing tests of theory is the most valuable quality an academic accountant can have.

43   It is impossible to view human behavior as a game or drama and be a serious academic accountant.

57   I would like to give more attention to synthesizing systematically the work of other accounting researchers.

66   A division of labor in which some accounting researchers specialize in theory, others in empirical research, is necessary for the growth of the discipline.

86   The major justification for any accounting research is that it generates accounting theory.

87   Some of the most powerful theories in accounting have emerged from the study of actual problems.

89   Accounting research is at its best when it takes an historical approach to a problem rather than a synthetic, timeless viewpoint.

III. Societal Role

10   Concern with immediate application of findings can often ruin potentially good accounting research.

12   The academic accountant contributes to the welfare of society mainly by providing an understanding of accounting practices, not through ideas for changing these.

15   Accountants should try to structure social institutions so as to maximize the satisfaction of individual needs.

16   Accounting theory for its own sake is good enough; it need not be applied.

18   Innovations in accounting theory must first be thoroughly developed and tested before we can begin to give them practical applications.

20   An applied accounting theory would be pointless unless it contributed to the development of theoretical (or basic) accounting theory.

22   The academic accountant, like any other intellectual, has the right and duty to criticize contemporary society.

29   The accountant has an obligation to help society in somewhat the same way in which the doctor is obliged to help his/her patient.

33   If I had more time, I would prefer to address myself to the solution of the daily problems of ordinary accounting practitioners.

45   Accounting researchers must take some responsibility for how their findings are used by others.

71   It is more important for a social scientist to understand social problems than to do what he/she can to cure them.

72   One part of the academic accountant's role is to be a critic of contemporary practice.

74   Unless accounting can at some point be relevant to the lives of ordinary people, it is socially useless.

78   One of the basic purposes of accounting is to help individuals cope with life in a complex society.

85   One of the social functions of accounting is to strive to increase the effectiveness of social institutions.

IV. Scientific Method

4   Academic accountants as researchers should view people merely as sources of data.

11   Use of statistics results in analyses that are better than those of direct observation.

17   Significant patterns of human behavior are too complex to be discovered by direct observation, but require the use of precise measurements.

21   Emphasis on methodology too often diverts accounting researchers from a study of accounting to the problem of how to study accounting.

27   The coming generation of academic accountants will need much more training in the use of higher mathematics.

60   Direct observation and intuitive insight are more fruitful for the accounting researcher than an emphasis on rigorous methodology.

79   In designing research, it is at least as important to be inventive as it is to be rigorous.

V. Value Freeness

3   Academic accountants do not really keep separate their personal experience and their professional work.

9   Active involvement in efforts to remedy social problems need not seriously bias an academic accountant.

19   Most academic accountants merely pay lip service to the ideal of being value free in their work, and are not really value free.

24   As teachers, academic accountants can express their personal values to students.

25   The more readily academic accountants accept research funds, the more will their value-free ideal be undermined.

31   Formulating a study in such a way as to get public financial support is a violation of professional integrity of an academic accountant.

44   The public expression of political values should always be avoided by academic accountants in their professional role.

51   Many social scientists are too prone to let foundations and government agencies determine the problems that they will study.

52   It seems likely that the more external support accounting research receives, the more politically conservative will the discipline become.

62   Much of current accounting theory is tacitly grounded in a conservative political ideology.

63   Its value-free ideal helps accounting research to remain independent of outside pressures and influences.

64   The subject matter of accounting makes it impossible to separate professional from nonprofessional values.

70   Accounting research will be unable to hold onto its value-free ideal in the face of increasing public demands for application of its findings.

VI. Professionalization

5   Accounting should be as much allied with the humanities as with the sciences.

6   The change of name from American Association of University Instructors in Accounting to American Accounting Association may be more consonant with the dignity of a professional organization.

28   The American Accounting Association is a learned society and any person with minimal qualifications should be allowed to join.

37   Some code of ethics for academic accountants should be promulgated and strictly enforced.

38   The notion is ridiculous that it will ever be necessary to license applied accounting researchers engaged in consulting on the basis of standardized examinations.

50   Once the American Accounting Association officially adopts a code of ethics, any members who deliberately violate the code ought to be dropped from the association.

56   It is impossible for the academic accountant to be fully competent without considerable knowledge of other social sciences.

61   Accountants will eventually need to take steps toward the licensing of applied accounting researchers, much like psychology has done.

82   Academic accountants should take steps to keep unqualified persons from belonging to the American Accounting Association and calling themselves accounting educators/researchers.

84   The worth of an academic accountant is best measured by the work of the people he/she teaches.

VII. Self-Image

30   Social science can aid both in achieving society's goals and in defining those goals.

32   The subject matter of accounting is at present ambiguous, vague, and elusive.

46   Social science is really the philosophy of the twentieth century.

58   Accounting is a body of scientific knowledge and theory; it is not a philosophy of life.

68   Accounting today deserves a more favorable public image than it has.

69   Modern societies could get along very well without the work of accountants.

75   Considering the extent of their contribution to science and society, academic accountants should be paid more.

81   There should be more formal prizes or awards available for academic accountants.

VIII. Prestige Criteria

1   Judgment of the scientific worth of a person is often distorted by appraisal of the number of his/her publications.

26   The pressure to publish has usually resulted in a flooding of the journals with inferior work.

40   It is understandable that those who do the most and best research should have greater prestige than the person who simply teaches well.

48   The best indicator of a person's professional worth is his/her scholarly publications.

53   To be a good teacher, an academic accountant must also be a good researcher.

IX. People and Politics

9   Active involvement in efforts to remedy social problems need not seriously bias an academic accountant.

36   Academic accountants often tend to become callously indifferent to human suffering.

49   Many academic accountants are unable to communicate and empathize with practitioners.

83   The academic accountant should not only think about communicating to his/her professional colleagues, but should also attempt to speak to a wider public.

88   Academic accountants should strive harder to write in a way that is more widely understandable.

INDEX

Abstracted empiricism, 25

Accounting: contempt for, 45; contextualism in, 11–12; formism in, 7–9; functionalist view in, 31–32; interpretive view in, 32–34; mechanism in, 9–11; organicism in, 12; radical humanist view in, 34–35; radical structuralist view in, 35–36; visions of multiple paradigm applied to, 51–53

Accounting knowledge: acquisition of, 105–8; conclusions regarding acquisition of, 117; Pepper's framework and, 1–7; visions in, 7–13

Accounting Principles Board (APB), 80

Accounting research: competing paradigms in, 45–46; conclusions about approaches to, 36–37; ideography vs. nomothesis in, 110–17; reality of, 17

Accounting researchers, classification of, 108–10

Accounting standard setting: legitimacy of process of, 72–74; need for, 75; objectives of, 71; procedures of, 71–72; products of, 69–70; theories of regulation and, 74–75

Accounting standard setting approaches:

Allison's, 83–84; conclusions regarding, 95; critical evaluations of, 93–95; free-market, 75–78; organizational process, 86–88; political, 88–93; private-sector, 78–81; public-sector, 81–83; rational actor, 84–86

Allison's approach to standard setting, 83–95. *See also* Accounting standard setting approaches

American Accounting Association (AAA), 121, 126

American Institute of CPAs (AICPA), 79, 89–90

Analytical Scientists, 109–10

Analytical/agency model, 54

Anarchistic individualism, 30

Anthropological/inductive paradigm, 53–54

Beaver, William, 12

Behavioral accounting research, 60

Behaviorism, 25

Behling, Orlando, 112, 115

Burrell, Gibson, 17, 18, 35

Capital-market efficiency theory, 59

Cheshire, J. D., 87

Committee on Accounting Procedures, 78
Comte, Auguste, 20
Conceptual Humanists, 110
Conceptual Theorists, 110
Conflict theory, 31
Contemporary Mediterranean Marxism, 31
Contextualism: in accounting, 11–12; explanation of, 1; World Hypotheses and, 5–6
Continuously contemporary accounting, 55
Cooper, David, 35
Critical theory: explanation of, 29, 30; Frankfurt School and, 29–30; Gramsci's sociology and, 29; Lukacsian sociology and, 29

Davis, T. R., 115
Decision-usefulness/decision-maker/aggregate-market-behavior paradigm, 57–59
Decision-usefulness/decision-maker/individual-user paradigm, 60–61
Decision-usefulness/decision-model paradigm, 56–57
Department of Energy (DOE), 91, 92
Deprival-value accounting, 55
Durkheim, Emile, 20, 24

Edey, H. C., 70
Elliot, R. K., 81
Energy Policy and Conservation Act, 85
Ethnography, paradigmatic, 115–16
Ethnomethodology, 28
Existential phenomenology, 27–28
Existentialism, 29

Federal Power Commission, 85
Federal Trade Commission, 91
Feroz, E. H., 87
Financial Accounting Standards Board (FASB): accounting standard setting and, 69, 78–81; Allison approach and, 93–95; due process procedures adopted

by, 71–72; legitimacy of, 73–74; objectives of, 85, 86; SEC and, 89–90, 92
Formism: in accounting, 7–9; explanation of, 1; World Hypotheses and, 3–4
Frankfurt school of social theory, 29
Free-market approach, 75–78
Functionalist view: in accounting, 31–32; explanation of, 20; in social sciences, 20, 24–25

Gramsci's sociology, 29

Hagstrom, W. O., 50
Hatfield, Henry Rand, 45
Hermeneutics, 26
Horngren, Charles, 80, 93

Ideographic approach: explanation of, 111; nomothesis approach vs., 111–17
Income smoothing/earnings management hypothesis, 54
Individualism, anarchistic, 30
Information economics, 54
Integrative theory, 25
Interactionism: explanation of, 24; phenomenological symbolic, 28; symbolic, 24–25
Interpretive view: in accounting, 32–34; explanation of, 25–26; social sciences, 26–28

Kaplan, Robert, 79
Kripke, Homer, 77–78
Kuhn, Thomas, 46, 49

Leftwich, R. W., 77
Lukacsian sociology, 29
Luthans, F. T., 115

Marx, Karl, 31
McCann, H. Gilman, 49
Mechanism: in accounting, 9–11; explanation of, 1; World Hypotheses and, 4–5
Merton, R. K., 50–51
Morgan, Gareth, 17, 18, 35

Natural science model, 110–11
Nomothesis approach: explanation of, 111–12; ideographic approach vs., 112–17

Objectivism, 25
Organicism: in accounting, 12; explanation of, 1; World Hypotheses and, 6–7
Organizational analysis approach, Burrell and Morgan's, 17–20
Organizational process model, 86–88

Paradigmatic ethnography, 115–16
Paradigms: anthropological/inductive, 53–54; components of, 52; decision-usefulness/decision-maker/aggregate-market-behavior, 57–59; decision-usefulness/decision-maker/individual-user, 60–61; decision-usefulness/decision-model, 56–57; definition of, 52; emergence of, 51; list of suggested, 53; Ritzer's visions of multiple, 51–53; true-income/deductive, 54–55
Particular Humanists, 110
Pepper, Stephen, 1–3, 6
Phenomenological sociology, 28
Phenomenological symbolic interactionism, 28
Phenomenology: existential, 27–28; explanation of, 27; transcendental, 27
Political approach, 88–93
Positive theory of accounting, 54
Predictive-ability criterion, 56
Present-value accounting, 55
Price-level-adjusted accounting, 55
Private-sector approach, 78–81
Public-sector approach, 81–83
Punctuated equilibrium paradigm, 46

Radical change, sociology of, 18
Radical humanist view: in accounting, 34–35; explanation of, 28; in social sciences, 28–30
Radical structuralist view: in accounting,

35–36; explanation of, 30–31; theories emerging from, 31
Rational actor model, 84–86
Reformulation, of World Hypotheses, 7
Regulation, sociology of, 18
Regulation theories, standard setting and, 74–75
Replacement-cost accounting, 55
Research: recognition as motivation for, 50. See also Accounting research
Ritzer, George, 51, 52
Russian social theory, 31

Schuetze, W., 81
Scientific revolutions, general theory of, 46, 49–51
Securities Act of 1933, 82; of 1934, 82
Securities and Exchange Commission (SEC), 82, 89–91
Social sciences: functionalist view of, 20, 24–25; interpretive view in, 25–28; nature of, 17–18; radical humanist view in, 28–30; radical structuralist view in, 30–31
Social-action theory, 25
Social-system theory, 24
Society, nature of, 18
Sociology: Gramsci's, 29; Lukacsian, 29; phenomenological, 28
Sociology of accounting: conclusions regarding, 140–41; hypotheses and methods of analysis and, 128–31, 134–39; overview of, 121; professional value system of academic accountants and, 123–27; value investigation and, 122–23; value measurement and, 127–28
Solipsism: explanation of, 26–27; as extreme approach, 29
Spencer, Herbert, 20
Spiegelberg, Herbert, 116
Standard setting: See Accounting standard setting
Statement of Financial Accounting Standards No. 2, 87, 88; No. 5, 87–88; No. 13, 88; No. 19, 84, 87 88

Sterling, Robert, 56
Structural functionalism, 24
Symbolic interactionism, 24–25
Systems theory, 24

Thevanaz, P. A., 27
Transcendental phenomenology, 27
True-income/deductive paradigm,
    54–55

Value system: of academic accountants,
    122–27; measurement issues related to,
    127–28; questionnaires regarding, 128–
    31, 134–39

World Hypotheses (Pepper): conclusions
    regarding, 12–13; contextualism and, 5–
    6; formism and, 3–4; mechanism and,
    4–5; nature of, 1–3; organicism and, 6–
    7; reformulation of, 7

About the Author

AHMED RIAHI-BELKAOUI is CBA Distinguished Professor of Accounting in the College of Business Administration, University of Illinois at Chicago. Author of more than 30 Quorum books and coauthor of several more, he is also a prolific author of articles published in the major scholarly and professional journals of his field, and has served on numerous editorial boards that oversee them.

ISBN 1-56720-100-8

HARDCOVER BAR CODE